The Life of D. L. MOODY

By

ARTHUR P. FITT

Foreword by

GEORGE SWEETING

MOODY PRESS
CHICAGO

ISBN: 0-8024-4727-9

CONTENTS

3

FOREWORD

THE YEARS 1973 and 1974 mark the 100th anniversary of the great evangelistic campaigns conducted by D. L. Moody and Ira D. Sankey throughout the British Isles. During this centenary observance, the Moody Bible Institute is pleased to reissue this biography of Moody, written by one who knew him best, his son-in-law, A. P. Fitt.

As you read this book, you will be impressed by the zeal and fervor of this great man of God. You will catch a glimpse of Moody's total dedication to Jesus Christ and of his burdened heart for the souls of men.

D. L. Moody was a man of unique ability and vision. In many ways he was far ahead of his time. The principles and techniques he employed in his work were often new and revolutionary. His dream for a school to train laymen to do the work of evangelism resulted in the establishment of the first Bible institute in the world. His intense desire to provide inexpensive literature to the public resulted in the founding of the Bible Institute Colportage Association, the first organization in North America to publish gospel books in paperback. Moody's emphasis upon practical Christian work came in a day when few people knew much about personal evangelism. His methods of soul-winning have since inspired thousands of Christians to become fishers of men.

Moody was also a pioneer in the field of mass evangelism. Many of the procedures he introduced and followed in his crusades throughout the United States and Europe have become standard practices for today's evangelistic campaigns. He has correctly been called "the father of modern mass evangelism."

Although he died nearly seventy-five years ago, the vision and work of Moody continues to the present. With a sense of urgency, Moody Bible Institute today is involved in many of the worldwide evangelistic efforts begun by Moody during the last century.

D. L. Moody was a man of great insight and vision. When he saw a need, he met it. When he discovered a new method of reaching men and women with the gospel, he used it for God's glory.

As you read the following pages, I trust that you, too, will discover the love and motivation that marked the life of this choice servant of God.

DR. GEORGE SWEETING
President
Moody Bible Institute

Chapter 1

EARLY LIFE AT NORTHFIELD

"Some day you will read in the papers that D. L. Moody, of East Northfield, is dead. Don't you believe a word of it! At that moment I shall be more alive than I am now. I shall have gone up higher, that is all; gone out of this old clay tenement into a house that is immortal, a body that death cannot touch, that sin cannot taint, a body like unto His own glorious body. I was born of the flesh in 1837. I was born of the Spirit in 1855. That which is born of the flesh may die. That which is born of the Spirit will live forever."

The words of D. L. Moody—his autobiography compressed into a few sentences. Between his birth, February 5, 1837, and his departure to be with Christ, December 22, 1899, there were crowded more, and more varied, experiences than fall to the general lot of men; and he firmly believed to the last that the opening portals of Heaven would only admit him to larger and truer service for his God and Saviour in unseen worlds.

By the grace of God he was what he was; but his life was largely influenced, under God, by his mother, Betsey Holton, born February 5, 1805. She came of old Puritan stock that had settled in Northfield, Massachusetts, as early as 1673. She married Edwin Moody on January 3, 1828. He was a mason by trade.

They had a comfortable home in Northfield, with an acre or two of land. Seven children were born to them. Dwight Lyman Ryther was the sixth, born on February 5, 1837.

On May 28, 1841, young Dwight was at school. A neighbor put his head in at the window, and asked if any of Ed Moody's children were there, saying that their father had just died suddenly. That morning he had gone about his work as usual; but a pain in his side sent him home to rest. About one o'clock in the afternoon he staggered to the bed, and was found dead a few minutes later, kneeling beside it as if in prayer.

The death of his father was the earliest thing that Dwight could remember. He could recall nothing about the funeral, but the shock of the sudden death made a lasting impression on him.

The widow was left in trying circumstances, which, however, only served to develop her sterling and heroic character. Her eldest child was only thirteen years old. Twins were born a month after her husband's death. He died a bankrupt, and she had no one on whom she could lean heavily for support.

When the neighbors would come in and tell her to bind out her children, she would say:

"Not as long as I have these two hands."

"Well," they would say, "you know one woman cannot bring up seven boys. They will turn up in jail, or with a rope around their necks."

She toiled on, and none of her children went to jail, or had a rope around his neck.

"If everyone had a mother like that mother," said Mr. Moody on the occasion of her funeral, "if the world was mothered by that kind of mother, there would be no need for jails."

The creditors swept away nearly everything, even the kindling. A snowstorm caused her to make the children stay in bed next morning until school-time, for want of wood to make a fire.

She was always bright and cheerful in the presence of her children, but that first year after her husband died she wept herself to sleep every night. Her sorrows drove her to God, and she claimed His promises for the fatherless and the widow.

In spite of all its privations, home was the sweetest place on earth to the Moody children. As long as that mother remained on earth, occupying that same home, but with all the comforts she desired, Dwight and her other children were drawn thither by the strong bands of love.

Dwight's early life differed little, in the main, from that of the ordinary New England boy. He continued to go to school in the winter, and learned the three R's and a little algebra. In the summer he "hired out." The first thing he did to earn money was to turn some neighbor's cows out to pasture on a mountain nearby, receiving a cent a day as wages.

Many anecdotes are told that prove that he was full of fun and loved practical jokes—a characteristic that he retained undiminished to the end. They indicate also those qualities of leadership which were so marked a feature of his later career.

At the closing exercises one school term, the boys gave recitations and dialogues. Dwight chose Mark Antony's oration over Caesar's body. He brought a box with him to serve as a coffin, and put it on the table. The audience, which included the local ministers, school committee, teachers, parents, and friends of the children, was moved to tears as he proceeded. Presently he lifted the cover of the box to take a last look at Caesar, and out jumped a tomcat!

"Scat!" shouted Dwight; and great was the uproar and laughter.

Some of the boys brought a pail to the cider-mill one afternoon, but not wishing to be seen carrying the cider home by daylight, they left it on one side until they should return later. Dwight had watched them, and when they were gone he got the pail and brought it home. One of his brothers thought he would add to the joke, so when suppertime came, he filled a glass with vinegar and set it at his own place at the table. Dwight fell into the trap. Supposing that his brother had helped himself to the cider, he reached over and proceeded to drink to the toast:

"Here's to the health of George Washington!"

But he enjoyed the joke himself.

On one occasion he wrote a notice summoning a temperance meeting in the schoolhouse on a given date, and signed a certain deacon's name in disguised handwriting. There was a crowded attendance, but no speaker appeared.

In that school district there were two parties. One party said that boys could not possibly be controlled without the cane, and they kept a school-master who acted on their plan; the other party said they should be controlled by love. The struggle went on, and at last, on one election day, the first party was put out and the other ruled in their stead. The boys said to each other that they were going to have a grand time that winter. There would be no more corporal punishment; they were going to be ruled by love.

The new teacher was a lady, and she opened the school with prayer. The boys hadn't seen that done before, and they were impressed, especially when she prayed that she might have grace and strength to rule with love. School went on for several weeks, and they saw no rattan.

Dwight, always the ringleader, was one of the first to break the rules. The teacher asked him to stay behind. He thought the cane was coming out again, and was in a fighting mood. She took him alone, sat down, and began to talk to him kindly. That was worse than the cane; he did not like it. She said:

"I have made up my mind that if I cannot control the school by love, I will give it up. I will have no punishment. If you love me, try to keep the rules."

Love conquered him, and he became a firm ally of that teacher.

When he was about eight years old, an incident happened that he ever afterward spoke of with gratitude. One of his elder brothers went to the town of Greenfield, twelve miles away, to work in a store for his board and attend school. He was so lonely that he found a place for Dwight. The incident can be best related in Mr. Moody's own words:

One cold day in November my brother came home, and said he had a place for me. I said I wouldn't go; but after it was talked over, they decided I should. That night was a long one.

The next morning we started. We went up on the hill and had a last sight of the old house. We sat down there and cried. I thought that would be the last time I should ever see that old home. I cried all the way down to Greenfield. There my brother introduced me to an old man who was so old that he could not milk his cows, and do the chores, so I was to do his errands, milk his cows, and go to school. I looked at the old man, and saw he was cross. I took a good look at his wife, and thought she was crosser than the old man. I stayed there an hour, and it seemed like a week. I went around then to my brother, and said:

"I am going home."

"What for?"

"I am homesick."

"Oh, well, you will get over it in a few days."

"I never will. I don't want to."

He said: "You will get lost if you start home now; it is getting dark."

I was frightened then, and I said: "I will go at daybreak tomorrow morning."

He took me to a shop window where they had some jackknives and other things, and tried to divert my mind. What did I care for those jackknives? I wanted to get back home to my mother and brothers; it seemed as if my heart was breaking.

All at once my brother said: "Dwight, here comes a man that will give you a cent."

"How do you know he will?" I asked.

"Oh, he gives every new boy that comes to town a cent."

I brushed away the tears, for I wouldn't have that man see me crying, and I got right into the middle of the sidewalk, where he couldn't help but see me, and kept my eyes right on him. I remember how that old man looked as he came tottering down the sidewalk. Oh, such a bright, cheerful, sunny face he had! When he came opposite to where I was, he stopped, took my hat off, put his hand on my head, and said to my brother:

"This is a new boy in town, isn't it?"

"Yes, sir, he is; just came today."

I watched to see if he would put his hand into his pocket. I was thinking of that cent. But he began to talk to me so kindly that I forgot all about it. He told me that God had an only Son, and He sent Him down here, and wicked men killed Him; and he said He died for me.

He talked only five minutes, but he took me captive. After he had given me this little talk, he put his hand into his pocket and took out a brand-new old-fashioned cent, a copper that looked just like gold. He gave me that. I thought it was gold, and didn't I hold it tight! I never felt so rich before or since. I don't know what became of that cent. I have always regretted that I didn't keep it; but I can feel the pressure of that old man's hand on my head today. Fifty years have rolled away, and I can hear those kind words ringing yet. I never shall forget that act.

At the age of sixteen, when he was still considered a small boy, he was taken one night to a lyceum meeting, where the townspeople had a debate. Toward the close of the meeting, when feeling was running high, he stood up, and in a few pointed impromptu sentences proved the weaker side in the debate to be right, and changed the current of the whole meeting.

He was immediately appointed leader of the next lyceum meeting, by acclamation, and went home feeling proud.

He selected as subject for the coming meeting the wrongs to which the Indians were subjected. He wrote out a speech of ten to fifteen minutes' duration, and for days his mother heard him tramping back and forth in his bedroom as he memorized this speech. When at last he appeared on the platform he recited the first few sentences, but memory failed him in his excitement, and he closed abruptly with the remark:

"The Indians went to the North Pole, and got froze up as stiff as steelyards."

He comforted a student of Mount Hermon School, of whom much had been expected, but who broke down during his final oration, by saying:

"Never mind! I broke down the first time I tried. You will get through the next time."

Naturally, you will inquire if Dwight showed any special aptitude in a religious direction during these early years. The answer must be no.

His mother was a religious woman—that quiet, home religion that characterized New England. She was then a Unitarian of the Channing school, differing very little in her beliefs from orthodox Congregationalists, and apparently having a vital faith in the widow's God. Northfield is not far from the scene of Jonathan Edward's revival labors, but the wave of his influence did not reach the Moodys.

About the only books in the home were a Bible and a book of devotions. Every morning Mrs. Moody read to her children from these. On Sunday all the children were sent to the Unitarian church, over a mile away, and they stayed through Sunday school. It was never a debatable question whether they should go or not. The boys used to go barefoot, carrying their shoes and stockings, and only putting them on when they came in sight of the church.

Mr. Everett, pastor of the Unitarian church, was very kind to the widow Moody in the days of her trial. At one time Dwight boarded with him and did his chores. But attendance at the Sunday services was irksome. Dwight could not understand the sermons. In fact, Sunday was a day the boys disliked, and at sundown—they began to observe Sunday at sundown on Saturday in those days—they would run out and throw up their caps, in jubilant spirits.

The only water baptism D. L. Moody received was at the hands of this Unitarian minister, but it was in the name of Father, Son, and Holy Ghost.

His mother tried to induce him to pray, but he said he had tried it, and it didn't work. Once, however, when he was about six years old, a rail fence fell on him. He could not extricate himself, and his cries for help were in vain, as he was too far away from any house. But he happened to think, "Maybe God will help me." So he prayed in his extremity, and believed that God answered his cry, as he was presently able to lift the rails.

One lesson the mother taught the boys was, that their word, once given, like the laws of the Medes, altered not. No excuse would ever be accepted for failure to perform a promise. The question she always asked was, "Did you say you would?" not, "Can you?" Once, when Dwight went to his brother George and sought release from an agreement to work for a neighbor for his board during the winter while he was also attending school, the case was carried to their mother. Dwight's cause of complaint was that for nineteen consecutive meals his only food had been milk and cornmeal, varied occasionally by the addition of some old crusts that were too hard for the family. When his mother found that he had enough to eat, such as it was, Dwight was sent back to keep his agreement.

Nothing that is recalled of his boyhood gives any reason to expect the large things that followed in Mr. Moody's life. But his love of harmless fun, his keen appreciation of a joke, even upon himself, his sensitive, compassionate nature, and his leadership of boy comrades were features which remained with him throughout the years that followed.

Chapter 2

BUSINESS AND CONVERSION IN BOSTON

As DWIGHT GREW OLDER he became ambitious for a change. The confines in which he found himself were too narrow. He began to appreciate the value of education, and tried to make the most of his schooling opportunities.

One day in the spring of 1854, when he was up in the woods cutting and hauling logs, he said to his brother Edwin, who was with him:

"I'm tired of this. I'm not going to stay 'round here any longer; I'm going off to get some other work."

He had two uncles in the boot and shoe business in Boston, of whom he sought work, but with little encouragement. Finally he left Northfield and went to Clinton, Massachusetts, where another brother was employed. He got a job in a book and stationery store, addressing wrappers for the first paper issued in that town; but he wasn't satisfied. Soon he went to Boston, where he had a homesick and trying time seeking work and finding none. At last he approached his uncles again, and was probably in such a condition that they were able to make their own terms with him. They agreed to take him into their store if he would promise to board at a place selected by them, to attend the

Mount Vernon Church and Sunday-school, and not to drink or gamble.

Dwight accepted the terms, and became the store boy, to do odds and ends. His ambition now was to make one hundred thousand dollars, and be a successful merchant. He spent his spare moments learning the prices of goods, and quietly familiarizing himself with the details of the business.

Although he was little acquainted with city ways and city manners, it soon became evident that he made up for deficiencies in polish and externals by a natural wit and brightness that lifted him out of his lowly position and brought him to the front as a salesman.

Letters that he wrote home at this time show that his boyish heart turned constantly toward Northfield. A postscript to a letter written to his mother on August 22, 1854, is characteristic of his correspondence. "Ho, George," he wrote, addressing his elder brother, "tell me what kind of a crop of corn this year, and potatoes also."

Nor did business so engross his attention as to crowd out the old tendency and liking for practical jokes. Before he had been in the store long, he settled on a tall cobbler, to plague him. One day he slit the leather seat of this cobbler's box, and placed a basin of water underneath. When the cobbler sat down, of course he got wet. This was repeated three times before the cobbler kicked the box over to see what was the matter. Immediately he grabbed a knife and started for young Moody, who was waiting on customers in the front part of the store. Moody was taking it all in, and rushed out into the street when he saw the cobbler coming.

One evening when he was aching for fun, a young man about his own age came along the sidewalk just as he was leaving the store. Moody stepped to his side and walked along with him, looking into his eyes all the time. The young man hurried; so did Moody. Finally the other commenced to run, and Moody kept up with him until the young man was thoroughly scared.

He had his share in all the legitimate excitement of the city. The abolition cause appealed strongly to him, and he attended stirring meetings in Faneuil Hall. He took part in the attack on the old courthouse to free the slave Anthony Burns. He used to tell how they took great planks to stave in the door, but when the soldiers fired and the crowd smelt powder, they backed away.

His first definite spiritual experience came to him during his stay in Boston—his conversion.

Attendance at church and Sunday school was obligatory, under agreement with his uncle—merely formal at first. There was many an Eliab, Abinadab, or Shammah on whom the anointing of the Spirit would more likely come than on this David.

Mount Vernon Church was organized as a revival church particularly to retain in Boston the fiery eloquence, holy zeal, and glowing fervor of Dr. Edward N. Kirk—just such a church as Mr. Moody's own church in Chicago later became. But the earnest cultured addresses of Dr. Kirk did not reach young Moody. It is said that he chose a seat in one of the obscurest pews in the gallery, and that, wearied with the hard work of the week, he used to sleep most of the time during the Sunday services.

In the Sunday school he was placed in a class taught by Edward Kimball. The teacher handed him a Bible, and told him the lesson was in John. Moody took the book, and hunted all through the Old Testament for John. The other young men (among whom were some Harvard students) detected his ignorance, and nudged each other. The teacher saw his embarrassment, and found the place for him. "I put my thumb in the place and held on," said Mr. Moody afterward; "I said then that if I ever got out of that scrape, I would not be caught there again." An incident that exhibits not merely his ignorance of the Bible, but also his dogged purpose to learn from his mistakes.

He gave close, respectful attention to his teacher from the first, and his demeanor in class was always earnest, quiet, and attentive. He seldom said anything. Once, when Mr. Kimball was teaching about Moses, trying to show that he was a man of self-control, wise and statesmanlike, who would have been at the head of affairs in any age or nation, Moody asked, with hesitancy:

"Mr. Kimball, don't you think Moses was *smart?*"

This word from his limited New England country vocabulary truly expressed Mr. Kimball's idea, and proved that he was anxious to grasp his teacher's meaning.

Before long, Mr. Kimball determined to speak to his new scholar about his spiritual condition. He went to Holton's shoestore one day, and found Moody in the back part of the store wrapping up shoes in paper and putting them on the shelves. Mr. Kimball told him of Christ's love and sacrifice. Evidently the young man was ripe for the Gospel message, although he had hardly felt that he had a soul till then. The light of Heaven flashed upon him, and never afterward grew dim.

How tenderly Mr. Moody used to refer to that transaction between himself and his Saviour! Preaching in Tremont Temple, early in 1898, he said:

"I can almost throw a stone from Tremont Temple to the spot where I found God over forty years ago. I wish I could do something to lead some young men to that same God. I wish I could make people understand what He has been to me. He has been a million times better to me than I have been to Him."

At other times he used to say: "The morning I was converted I went outdoors and fell in love with everything. I never loved the bright sun shining over the earth so much before. And when I heard the birds singing their sweet songs, I fell in love with the birds. Everything was different."

The natural zeal and energy of the man at once sought to find expression in service for the new Master whose cause he had entered. One of the first things he did was to go before the church committee with a view to joining the church. He was then only eighteen years old. He had been in Mr. Kimball's class only a few months. The committee was composed of earnest, sympathetic men (among them Mr. Kimball), who made the examination very carefully and gently, knowing young Moody's limited knowledge and hesitation. The questions had to be shaped so that the answers would be simply "yes" or "no." At length one of the deacons asked: "Mr. Moody, what has Jesus Christ done for you, and for us all, that specially entitles Him to our love and obedience?"

The question embarrassed him. It was too long and too wordy for him to answer promptly, but he said: "I think He has done a good deal for all of us, but I don't think of anything He has done in particular as I know of."

Nothing, therefore, was elicited at this examination that could be considered satisfactory evidence of conversion. Under the circumstances the committee deferred recommending him for admission to the church. Three of their number were appointed to take care of his case, and to seek to open up to him the way of God more plainly. When he came before the committee again, no more doctrinal questions were asked of him than previously; but his earnest desire to be among God's people, and the feeling that he would get more good in the church than from being either refused or delayed admission, and the conviction that he would do no harm in the church anyway, although he was still unable to give any intelligent information as to his religious experience—these reasons led to his being accepted for membership March 12, 1856.

Mr. Moody never complained of the action of the committee in this case. On the contrary, he thought they had done the wise and proper thing. He was very solicitous in later years about persons being admitted to membership in our churches without having really been born again, and directed his efforts to bring men and women face to face with this question, to see not only if they had become partakers of the divine nature, but also that with Paul they should be able to say: "I *know* whom I have believed, and *am persuaded* that he is able to keep that which I have committed to him."

Stories are current—whether true or not it is impossible to verify in every case, although in some instances they are known to be false—of one and another trying to rebuke young Moody for speaking at prayer meetings, and seeking to repress his zeal. It can easily be credited that he was whole-hearted and active in religion just as he was in other things. But Mr. Kimball, whose loving interest in his Sunday-school pupil never abated, says that while Moody attended the Friday evening church prayer meetings quite regularly, he has no recollection of hearing him speak except a few times, when he was invited by the leader of the meeting to take part. "I can truly say (and in saying it I magnify the infinite grace of God as bestowed upon Mr. Moody)," wrote Mr. Kimball, "that I have seen few persons whose minds were spiritually darker when he came into my Sunday-school class, or one who seemed more unlikely ever to become a Christian of clear, decided views of Gospel truth, still less to fill any sphere of extended public usefulness." Dr. Kirk and the church officers lived to thank God for Mr. Moody's marvelous development in grace and in the knowledge and service of our Lord and Saviour Jesus Christ.

Chapter 3

EARLY CHICAGO CAREER

"CHICAGO, September 20, 1856.—I reached this far-famed city of the West one week ago, in the night. . . . I went into a prayer meeting last night, and as soon as I made myself known I had friends enough. After meeting they came to me, and seemed to be as glad to see me as if I were their earthly brother. God is the same here as He was in Boston, and in Him I can find peace. . . . I wish you could have seen a couple of ladies that came on with me. I was introduced to them at the depot in Boston. They were such good Christians. They stayed here until Friday night, and then went South, and I felt as if Christ was the only friend I had in Chicago. But since then I have found some nice people. . . ."

These extracts are from the first letter D. L. Moody wrote to his mother after reaching Chicago.

His ambition had been stirred by the opening up of the great West. Boston proved too conservative for him. He was not comfortable in his surroundings, and privately decided to strike out where there was more room for a young man with push and enthusiasm to succeed in business. His home folks were opposed to his going to the then faraway city of Chicago, but he wrote his mother that if God would bring him there, he would devote his whole life to His service. While he undoubtedly did not mean this to imply giving up business, as his ambition was still to become a successful merchant, it shows how ready he was to follow God's leading, and make his whole life tell for Christ.

After reaching Chicago, he secured employment in Wiswall's boot and shoe store. Though personal appearances were still against him, his ability as a salesman soon asserted itself. He became popular with the rougher class of customers, and used to take special delight in handling difficult people.

After a time, when Wiswall added a jobbing department to his business, Moody found himself still more in his element. It gave him a chance to push out in his own interests, to exercise his tireless energies outside the routine of the store. He used to visit the depots, and inspect the hotel registers for incoming visitors. When the store closed at night, he would accost passersby and try to sell them rubbers or other seasonable goods. He was all the time on the lookout for customers.

On December 16, 1856, he wrote his brother Samuel at Northfield as follows:

> I suppose you would like to know how I am doing. Well, I am doing first-rate. Shall be on there in the summer, if not before. I came very near going last week. A man offered to pay my fare if I would go with him to buy some goods, but Mr. Wiswall was so driven for help that he could not spare me. I should like to come back to the Bay State once more. Things don't look out here much as they do in Boston. A good many

of the stores are kept open on the Sabbath-day. It is a great holiday out here.

The same day he wrote his mother:

> I have made thirty dollars a week ever since I came out here. . . . Don't let Uncle Samuel get hold of it, but as it has turned out, I have done the very best thing in coming out here. My expenses are a good deal, but I can make more money here than in Boston. I will send you a bill of fare of the house where I board, and then you can judge whether I shall starve or not.

One joke that Mr. Moody used to tell about himself with great enjoyment occurred at this period.

It was during President Lincoln's first presidential campaign, and Mr. Moody was traveling through southern Illinois. The train had stopped at a small village. A farmer was sauntering up and down the platform, and as he came opposite Mr. Moody's window the latter asked him if he knew that Lincoln was on the train. The man showed great interest, and said:

"No! Is he?"

"I don't think he is," answered Mr. Moody. "I only asked you if you knew that he was."

The farmer said nothing, but continued his walk on the platform. As he came opposite the window again he remarked that their town had had some excitement.

"What's the matter?" Mr. Moody asked.

"The authorities wouldn't let some folks bury a woman," replied the farmer.

"Why not?"

"She wasn't dead," was the laconic reply.

The first Sunday he was in Chicago he attended the morning Sunday-school in the First Baptist Church. His future wife sat there among the pupils, a girl in her teens. He brought with him a letter to the Plymouth Congregational Church, with which he immediately identified himself. Here he undertook his earliest form of Christian activity. He realized that there were many young men in this growing Western city, away from home and friends as he was, and who felt diffidence about attending churches where the pews were all engaged. He therefore rented four pews in Plymouth Church, and invited young men to attend and sit in his pew, a form of ministry that he prosecuted with unusual success.

At this time he also joined the Young Men's Mission Band of the First Methodist Episcopal Church, whose purpose was to visit hotels and boarding-houses on Sunday mornings, distributing tracts and inviting people to the church services.

Sunday afternoons he devoted to a little mission Sunday-school on the corner of Chicago Avenue and Wells Street. He offered to take a class. The superintendent said he had twelve teachers already and only sixteen scholars, but if he could work up a class of his own, he would be welcome. Next Sunday Moody appeared with eighteen ragged, dirty "hoodlums," gathered off the streets, but each nonetheless needing to be saved. Turning these children over to some of the other teachers, Moody sought out more scholars, until he filled the school to overflowing. He had no idea that he himself could teach, but devoted to God his one talent of being able to "drum up" recruits, both young men and children, for the services of the house of God.

While Mr. J. B. Stillson, of Rochester, New York was at this time engaged in the erection of the old Chicago custom-house, he used to distribute tracts and hold meetings along the river. One day he met Moody, who struck him as "a young man of earnest purpose, plain habits, and not very much education." The two became co-workers in scattering religious reading among sailors, in saloons and boarding houses, and in hundreds of poor families living in that portion of the city known as "the Sands," on the north side of the city, extending from the jail to the lake.

Letters written home at this period prove that he was rapidly ripening in Christian experience, however little he knew of correct doctrine. Writing to his brother George, on March 17, 1857, he said:

> I can make more money here in a week than I could in Boston in a month. But that is not all. I have enjoyed more religion here than ever in my life. George, I hope you will hold on to the promises in the Bible. I find the better I live the more enjoyment I have, and the more I think of God and His love the less I think of this world's troubles. George, don't let anything keep you from the full enjoyment of God's love. I think we have things sometimes come upon us to try our faith, and God likes to see us cling on. As the psalmist says in one place, God likes to chastise them whom He loves. So let us pray for each

other, for I think it becomes Christians to pray for each other. I have brought you before God in my prayers, and I hope you have done the same for me.

A year later (May 21, 1858) he wrote his mother as follows:

I have a good situation, and I mean to work my cards to make it better. I have been very successful so far, and if nothing happens I will do well. Luther [his brother] thought I was very foolish in my leaving Wiswall's, but I have got me a situation that is worth five of that. If I have my health, and my God is with me, I shall succeed better here in Chicago than I ever thought. Mother, I hope you will not forget to pray for your son here in the West, surrounded by temptations on all sides. I never worked in a place since my conversion that there were so many wild young men as here. I hope you will plead with God that I may live a consistent Christian before them, that they may not lead me astray. I am in hopes to live so before them that I may succeed in winning their souls to Christ. Pray for me, dear mother.

In the fall of 1858, Mr. Moody started a Sunday-school of his own in a vacant saloon, his helpers being Mr. Stillson and a Mr. Carter, who led the singing. Larger quarters were immediately needed, and when the mayor of the city understood the plan for trying to save the children in the submerged portion of the city, he gladly gave the use of the North Market Hall for Sunday-school work.

This was a large hall over a market, owned by

the city, and rented nearly every Saturday night for
balls, when liquor and refreshments and cigars were
freely used. It was commodious and convenient to
that tough quarter in which Mr. Moody delighted
to work.

Seeking out some of the street arabs who did not
like the Wells Street mission school and had therefore dropped out, Mr. Moody invited them to *assist*
him in his new venture. The boys were pleased to
become partners, and willingly entered upon the
work. One of those boys subsequently became post-
master of Chicago and commander-in-chief of the
Grand Army of the Republic.

In preparing the hall for balls, the chairs, class
banners, and other furniture used by Mr. Moody
were thrown into a miscellaneous heap at one end
of the hall. He and his "partners"—used, therefore,
to get around at 6 A.M. Sunday mornings to sweep
out the hall, remove the beer-barrels, cigar-stumps,
and other debris of the ball, and rearrange their
furniture and banners for the 3 P.M. service. Sweep-
ing the floors was in his eyes as true service for God
as superintending the school.

Mr. Moody's genius was taxed to keep control.
The boys indulged in all sorts of catcalls, whistling,
etc., while there was no semblance of classes.

One Sunday Mr. John V. Farwell came by invitation to visit the school.

About half of the boys rushed forward to shine
his shoes as he came in. Presently Mr. Moody invited him to make a speech, at the close of which
he was elected superintendent of the school by acclamation, to his utter surprise.

Said Mr. Moody to one man: "I want you to teach these lambs."

"*Lambs? Wolves,* you mean!" replied the other.

Mr. Moody or some helper would read a passage of Scripture, sing a hymn, tell an anecdote—anything to fill up the time. By degrees the school increased to fifteen hundred, and as new teachers enlisted, order was achieved out of chaos. It was before the day of International Lessons, however, and scholars and teachers simply had their common textbook, the New Testament. Denominational lines were not recognized.

Mr. Moody's devices for running the school were eminently successful.

He issued stock certificates of the "North Market Sabbath-school Association; capital, ten thousand dollars; forty thousand shares at twenty-five cents each." These certified the purchase of shares "for the erection of a new building." "For dividends apply at the school each Sabbath at 3 p.m."

His plan for disposing of unfit teachers was automatic. Scholars were allowed, by permission of the superintendent, to transfer from one class to another. The inevitable result was that teachers who failed to interest their scholars were speedily left without classes.

When he bought an Indian pony in order to save time in making calls, he used to let the boys ride the pony while he was indoors.

He used to make much of picnics, entering into the sports with as great zest as the youngest. He was then a very fast runner. At one picnic he picked up a barrel partly filled with apples, and holding it so that the apples would spill out, he ran ahead, followed by the boys. One of the latter ran in front of him, and lay down on the ground, so that Mr. Moody, who was watching the apples, fell over him.

Thirteen street arabs were promised a new suit each at Christmas if they would attend regularly every Sunday until that time. Their nicknames were: Red Eye, Smikes, Madden the Butcher, Jackey Candles, Giberick, Billy Blucannon, Darby the Cobbler, Butcher Lilroy, Greenhorn, Indian, Black Stovepipe, Old Man, Ragbreeches Cadet. All but one fulfilled the conditions. Mr. Moody had them photographed "before" and "after," the pictures being known by the titles, "Will it pay?" and "It does pay!" This uniformed group became known as "Moody's bodyguard."

Thirteen years later a friend called at a railway ticket office. The agent asked him to step inside, and said: "You do not seem to know me?"

"No, I have not that pleasure."

"You know 'Moody's bodyguard'?"

"Yes; I have a picture of them in my home."

"Well," said the agent, "when you go home, take a square look at the ugliest of the lot, and you will see your humble servant, now a church member and heir to Mr. Moody in that work."

One of his first principles was that the worse the boy was, the more reason against ejecting him. Hence expulsion was never thought of.

One young bully of fifteen years was especially noisy and troublesome, and all the usual means failed to tame him. At last Mr. Moody said to Mr. Farwell: "If that boy disturbs his class today, and

you see me go for him and take him into the anteroom, you ask the school to rise and sing a very
loud hymn until I return."

The program was executed as arranged. Mr.
Moody seized the boy, hurried him into the anteroom before he realized what was happening, and
locked the door. He gave the boy a terrible thrash-
ing, and presently returned, with face flushed, but
wearing an expression of victory.

Said he, "I believe that boy is saved."

The boy was converted soon afterward, and years
later acknowledged that he was still enjoying the
benefits of that Gospel exercise.

The neighboring Roman Catholic children were
a source of great trial to Mr. Moody, disturbing
his meetings and breaking windows in the hall.
When all other resources had failed to stop this
vandalism, he went to see Bishop Duggan. He
called at the bishop's residence, and was told the
bishop was not in.

"Then I'll wait for him," said he.

By and by the two met and he stated his complaint, and requested the bishop to exercise control over his parishioners. The bishop met him
kindly, but said a man of his zeal ought to be inside the true church. Mr. Moody said he wanted to
be right, but that if he became a Roman Catholic,
he would have to give up his noon prayer meeting.

"No, you won't," said the bishop.

"But I couldn't pray with Protestants!"

"Yes, you could."

"Then," said Mr. Moody, "if a Roman Catholic
can pray with a Protestant, won't you kneel down

right here and pray that God may open our eyes
to the truth?"

They knelt and prayed together, and as a result
of that interview Mr. Moody had no more organized persecution from his neighbors.

When Abraham Lincoln was president-elect he
spent a Sunday in Chicago, and visited the school on
Mr. Farwell's invitation, on condition that he
should not be asked to make a speech. When the
boys learned who he was, their enthusiasm burst
all restraints. As Lincoln rose to leave, Mr. Moody
announced the conditions of his visit, but added:

"If Mr. Lincoln finds it in his heart to say a few
words for our encouragement, of course we will
listen attentively."

Thus taken, Mr. Lincoln made a helpful address,
based upon his own early experiences. He earnestly admonished the boys to be attentive to their
teachers and put in practice what they learned, and
by so doing some day, perhaps, any one of them
might become President of the United States.

An older brother of one pupil was in the South.
On hearing of Mr. Moody's influence over his family, he wrote home that he would "whip Moody
within an inch of his life" on his return. When he
got back he was taken down with typhoid fever,
and Mr. Moody helped to nurse him. The man
was so touched that his wrath disappeared, he became converted, and remained a firm friend of the
work.

One day a forgetful or careless scholar took his
seat with his cap on. One of "Moody's bodyguard"
discovered him, planted a stunning blow between

his eyes, and sent him sprawling to the floor, with the remark:

"I'll teach you not to enter Moody's Sunday school with your hat on."

On one of his recruiting excursions Mr. Moody reached a house where there were not only children, but also a jug of whisky, which the father had laid in for Sunday. Mr. Moody got the whisky and emptied it into the street. Next week when he returned, bent on a similar errand, the man was awaiting him. As he confessed to demolishing the whisky-jug, the man took off his coat to fight him. But Mr. Moody said:

"I emptied the jug for the good of yourself and your family. If I am to be thrashed for it, let me pray for you all before you do it."

Falling on his knees, he prayed earnestly for father, mother, and children, as he had learned to pray under such circumstances. When he rose from his knees the father's anger had cooled down, and he was permitted to have the children for his school.

Writing to a brother at Northfield from La Crosse, Wisconsin, on July 18, 1859, he said:

> How are you getting along with your Sunday-school, and who is superintendent of it now? and how large a school have you got? Tell me all about it. If I were in your place, I would not have it stopped every winter, but keep it a-going. I shall expect to have a good time next Sunday when I get home, for I have been away some time now, and the children are so glad to see me when I return. I think I have got the best school

there is in the West; anyway, it is the largest school this side of New York. I wish you could see it.

Mr. Moody loved his school, and his scholars loved him. Many of them were as brands plucked from the burning, and were knit to him by the common love of God which had been shed abroad in their hearts. One scholar moved to another part of the city. The little fellow kept up his attendance, although it meant a long, tiresome walk each way. Someone asked him why he went so far, and said that there were plenty of other schools just as good nearer his home.

"They may be as good for others, but not for me," was the boy's reply.

"Why not?"

"Because they love a fellow over there," he replied.

"If only we could make the world believe that we love them," said Mr. Moody, "there would be fewer empty churches and a smaller proportion of our population who never darken a church door. Let *love* replace *duty* in our church relations, and the world will soon be evangelized."

Chapter 4

HOW HE CAME TO GIVE UP BUSINESS

IN 1860 MR. MOODY was led to give up business and devote all his time to Christian work.

In addition to the Sunday school held on Sunday afternoons in the North Market Hall, he used to hold Sunday evening services for the boys in a smaller room connected with the hall. From the beginning he taught the importance of confessing Christ as one's Saviour, of giving testimony as to Christian experience, and also of engaging in active work. Later on these evening meetings multiplied, as parents became interested. During the week Mr. Moody spent much time daily in visiting in the homes of the scholars.

As a result of the revival of 1857-58, the YMCA was organized in Chicago. A daily noon prayer meeting, similar to the Fulton Street prayer meeting in New York, was held. Mr. Moody used to attend. At first there was not much general interest in it, but being aroused to action by the example of an old Scotchman who was the only attendant one day, when he went through the program of hymn, prayer, and Scripture reading all alone, Mr. Moody and others began to work up the attendance, and very soon the meeting was flourishing.

Meanwhile, he prosecuted his boot and shoe business with unabated zeal and unfailing success. Events succeeded each other that had important bearings on his future. After two years with Mr. Wiswall, he had found employment as a commercial traveler for Mr. C. N. Henderson, a gentleman who was interested in the North Market Hall work. This position gave him greater liberty for mission work, as his time was now his own, he worked on commission, and could get away without encroaching upon his employer's rights to his time.

A letter he wrote home under date of January 2, 1859, shows his feeling toward Mr. Henderson:

> On my return from the country last week I found my hopes all vanished. The one whom I had looked to for advice and counsel, and had proved to be more than a friend to me, was dead. . . . That man was my employer, Mr. Henderson. I shall miss him very much. He was the truest friend I have met since I left home. He seemed to take as much interest in my welfare as he would in the welfare of his own son.

The confidence in which Mr. Moody was held was shown when a year later Mrs. Henderson insisted that he settle up their business. A young man of only twenty-three years, he shrank from the responsibility of handling an estate that was so large; but "I feel greatly honored," he wrote his mother, "for they had a great many friends who are good businessmen. I never have been put in so responsible a position in my life, and my prayer is that I may do myself credit. I am in hopes that you will not forget to pray for me, for I am nothing without the same God that has been with me since I started out in life. Do not say anything about this, will you?"

Results proved that Mrs. Henderson's confidence was not misplaced.

He next found employment with the firm of Buel, Hill & Granger, devoting a large share of every day to visitation and other work connected with his Sunday-school, while meetings multiplied still more at night. Before a year elapsed, he cut loose altogether from business.

The story may be told in his own words:

I had never lost sight of Jesus Christ since the first night I met Him in the store at Boston, but for years I really believed that I could not work for God. No one had ever asked me to do anything.

When I went to Chicago, I hired four pews in a church, and used to go out on the street and pick up young men and fill these pews. I never spoke to those young men about their souls; that was the work of the elders, I thought. After working for some time like that, I started a mission Sunday school. I thought numbers were everything, and so I worked for numbers. When the attendance ran below one thousand, it troubled me; and when it ran to twelve or fifteen hundred, I was elated. Still none was converted; there was no harvest.

Then God opened my eyes.

There was a class of young ladies in the school who were without exception the most frivolous set I ever met. One Sunday the teacher was ill, and I took that class. They laughed in my face, and I felt like opening the door and telling them all to get out and never come back.

That week the teacher of the class came into the store where I worked. He was pale, and looked very ill.

"What is the trouble?" I asked.

"I have had another hemorrhage of my lungs. The doctor says I cannot live on Lake Michigan, so I am going to New York State. I suppose I am going home to die."

He seemed greatly troubled, and when I asked he reason he replied: "Well, I have never led any of my class to Christ. I really believe I have done the girls more harm than good."

I had never heard anyone talk like that before, and it set me thinking.

After awhile I said: "Suppose you go and tell them how you feel. I will go with you in a carriage, if you want to go."

He consented, and we started out together. It was one of the best journeys I ever had on earth. We went to the house of one of the girls, called for her, and the teacher talked to her about her soul. There was no laughing then! Tears stood in her eyes before long. After he had explained the way of life, he suggested that we have prayer. He asked me to pray. True, I had never done such a thing as to pray God to convert a young lady there and then. But we prayed, and God answered our prayer.

We went to other houses. He would go upstairs, and be all out of breath, and he would tell the girls what he had come for. It wasn't long before they broke down and sought salvation.

When his strength gave out, I took him back to his lodgings. The next day we went out again. At the end of ten days he came to the store with his face literally shining.

"Mr. Moody," he said, "the last one of my class has yielded herself to Christ."

I tell you we had a time of rejoicing.

He had to leave the next night, so I called his class together that night for a prayer meeting, and there God kindled a fire in my soul that has never gone out. The height of my ambition had been to be a successful merchant. If I had known that meeting was going to take that ambition out of me, I might not have gone. But how many times I have thanked God since for that meeting!

The dying teacher sat in the midst of his class, and talked with them, and read the fourteenth chapter of John. We tried to sing "Blest Be the Tie that Binds," after which we knelt to pray. I was just rising from my knees when one of the class began to pray for her dying teacher. Another prayed, and another, and before we rose the whole class had prayed. As I went out I said to myself: "O God, let me die rather than lose the blessing I have received tonight!"

The next evening I went to the depot to say good-by to that teacher. Just before the train started, one of the class came, and before long, without any prearrangement, they were all there. What a meeting that was! We tried to sing, but we broke down. The last we saw of that dying teacher he was standing on the platform of the rear car, his finger pointing upward, telling us to meet him in Heaven.

I didn't know what this was going to cost me. I was disqualified for business; it had become distasteful to me. I had got a taste of another world, and cared no more for making money. For some days after, the greatest struggle of my life took place. Should I give up business and give myself wholly to Christian work, or should I not? God helped me to decide aright, and I have never regretted my choice. Oh, the luxury of leading someone out of the darkness of this world into the glorious light and liberty of the Gospel!

The last eight months he spent in business he made five thousand dollars—quite a large sum in those days. The first year in Christian work he did not receive more than three hundred dollars! But he never wavered. He believed Christ would provide the means as long as He had use for him. It meant living on crackers and cheese, sleeping on benches and settees in the YMCA hall, and other "hardships." Through all his privations he remained steadfast to the commission he knew he had received from on high.

When his purpose became known, he was dubbed "Crazy Moody." Later, when his efforts proved successful, and he became one of the leading religious factors of the city and of the Northwest, he became "Brother Moody." Later still, when his reputation extended over two continents, his title became "Mr. Moody," and plain "Mr. Moody" or "D. L. Moody" as he remained until his coronation.

He was now free to prosecute with greater activity the many labors entailed by his Sunday-school and his new love, the YMCA. Under his leadership the latter became, like the former, a live popular institution, whose influence was soon felt throughout the city.

He never received a regular salary from any source after leaving business.

Chapter 5

MISSIONARY AND PASTORAL LABORS IN CHICAGO

MOST OF THE CHILDREN who attended the North Market Hall were gathered from homes where there was no Christian influence or training. Mr. Moody felt (as he expressed it) that he had the children an hour a week and the Devil had them the rest of the time. That led him to start the Sunday night meetings, and as interest increased he was forced, and not unwillingly, to open up every night. Presently it was necessary to find larger quarters than the small anteroom occupied Sunday nights. He hired a corner store that had been used as a saloon, fitted it up conveniently, and held meetings every night for prayer and exhortation.

The tide kept coming in, and as converts increased it became a serious question what to do with them. Mr. Moody tried to get them to join existing churches, but the poorer classes felt strange and out of place in the beautiful edifices. Besides, they had an affection for the place where they had first been blessed, and the rough and ready methods of Mr. Moody suited them better than the more deliberate proceedings of the ordinary church service. Most of the converts had no religious antecedents;

they had no preference for one denomination rather than another. The tie that bound them to the mission could not exist toward any church.

It was inevitable that some permanent organization should be founded. Mr. Moody undertook to provide a building suitable for their needs. The outcome was the Illinois Street Church.

This building was adapted for Sunday school as well as church purposes. It held fifteen hundred people in the main hall, and also had several classrooms.

It was dedicated early in 1864, and became one of the most thriving and active churches in the city. Mr. Moody was a deacon, and deacons and members alike were kept hard at work. In addition to ordinary meetings, there were also special meetings for men, young men, and boys; for mothers and girls; Bible, Gospel, praise, prayer, and testimony meetings; without mentioning special cases, such as watch-night and thanksgiving services. Besides all these, cottage meetings were held at the homes of the members, and open-air meetings. The church building was almost in constant use, and Mr. Moody was the life and moving spirit of all. It was the scene of continuous revival activity and zeal.

It became his custom to preach at the Sunday morning service, and conduct the Sunday school (numbering a thousand scholars and upward) in the afternoon. In the evening he repeated his morning address at Farwell Hall, with an inquiry meeting following, while some visiting minister or friend conducted the meeting at the church.

Mr. Moody never let a man pass by without getting him to preach, if he were able. This happy faculty of enlisting others brought him into close personal touch with most of the leading Christian workers who came to Chicago, among whom may be mentioned Dr. Punshon and John Darby, of England.

Mr. Moody was in growing demand as a speaker at Sunday school and YMCA conventions. He and his fellow laborers used to take these by storm and sweep away all rules, with the result that as often as not the convention work would be swallowed up in a revival.

"I have been to prayer meetings every night but two for eight months," he wrote his mother as early as June 5, 1861. "The Lord is blessing my labors, and I think you would say, 'God bless you, go forward.' . . . I was away all last week to Sunday school conventions. Have got to go again this week, and all of next week, so you see I am driven more than I ever was in my life. I have crowded houses wherever I go. Last week the house was full, and the sidewalk outside, so they had to open another church, and I had to speak in two houses. The Lord blessed me very much, and the work commenced in good earnest, so they have sent for me again. O Mother, if you could be out here you never would be sorry I gave up my business, for if I had not I suppose I should have lost everything I was worth, for all but one or two merchants in the boot and shoe trade have failed. . . ."

Many anecdotes might be related to illustrate his direct method of approach on religious questions.

One night, on his way home, he saw a man leaning against a lamppost. Stepping up to him and placing his hand on his shoulder, he said:

"Are you a Christian?"

The man flew into a rage, doubled up his fist, and got ready to pitch Mr. Moody into the gutter.

The latter said: "I am very sorry if I have offended you, but I thought I was asking a proper question."

"Mind your own business!" roared the other.

"That is my business," he answered.

About three months later, on a bitter cold morning about daybreak, someone knocked at Mr. Moody's door.

"Who's there?" he asked, "and what do you want?"

"I want to become a Christian," was the reply.

He opened the door, and to his astonishment there was the man who had cursed him for accosting him as he leaned against the lamppost!

Said he: "I haven't had any peace since that night. Your words have haunted and troubled me. I couldn't sleep last night, and I thought I'd come and get you to pray with me."

That man accepted Christ, and the moment he had done so, asked:

"What can I do for Him?"

He taught in the Sunday school until the war broke out, when he enlisted, and was one of the first to be shot down, but not before he had given a ringing testimony for God.

At one town Mr. Moody visited, he asked to be taken to the home of the worst man in the place.

They sent him to the home of an infidel carpenter, whose wife, however, was a Christian. He went into the man's shop, and asked him:

"Do you know that Jesus of Nazareth was a carpenter?"

"No," was the surly answer; "I don't know, and don't care."

But Mr. Moody was interested in him, and before leaving town told the carpenter's wife that her husband would be converted. Said he:

"I'll be passing through here in two days on the train. Won't you signal me if he has come into the light?"

When the time came, he had the joy of seeing the woman standing on the porch of her house, which stood near the track, excitedly waving a large white tablecloth.

An overzealous critic, who was not an overactive worker, took Mr. Moody to task for his defects in speech, in the early days.

"You oughtn't to speak in public," he said; "you make so many mistakes in grammar."

"I know I make mistakes," was the reply, "and I lack a great many things; but I'm doing the best I can with what I've got. But look here, friend, you've got grammar enough; what are you doing with it for Jesus?"

On one occasion Mr. Moody was one of several speakers at a convention. A minister who followed him took occasion in his speech to criticize him, saying that his address was made up of newspaper clippings, etc. When he sat down, Mr. Moody was one of several speakers at a convention. A min-

ister who followed him took occasion in his speech
to criticize him, saying that his address was made
up of newspaper clippings, etc. When he sat down,
Mr. Moody stepped to the front again, and said he
recognized his want of learning and his inability to
make a fine address; he thanked the minister for
pointing out his shortcomings, and asked him to
lead in prayer that God would help him to do better.

He once heard someone say:

"The world has yet to see what God can do *with*,
and *for*, and *through*, and *in* a man who is fully and
wholly consecrated to Him."

The statement took hold of him. He thought to
himself: "He did not say a great man, or a learned
man, or a rich man, or an eloquent man, or a clever
man; simply a man. Well, I am a man. It lies
with the man himself whether he will or will not
make that full and entire consecration. I will try
my utmost to be that man."

That spirit was evidently animating him. Letters written at this period of his life exhibited his
inner purposes.

"Tell all my friends," he wrote home on February 12, 1861, "there is nothing like the religion
of Jesus Christ. I am in hopes the family altar is
kept up at home. . . ."

"I hope you will do all you can personally for
your Saviour," he wrote to his brother Sam, February 13, 1865. "Talk for Him. Pray to Him.
Labor for Him, and do all things for Him, and the
good Lord will never leave you. Read often the
fourteenth chapter of John."

The wideness of his charity was illustrated by his conduct toward a man who used to attend the noon prayer meetings and open-air meetings in order to make disturbance. Even Mr. Moody could not suppress him. While he stood at the door shaking hands with people at the close of the prayer meeting one day, this man came along. After a moment's hesitation, Mr. Moody stretched out his hand, and said:

"I suppose if Jesus Christ could eat the Last Supper with Judas Iscariot, I ought to shake hands with you."

Chapter 6

HOW MR. MOODY PREPARED
HIS SERMONS

FOR YEARS he never expected to do more in the way of preaching than to give five- or ten-minute addresses to his Sunday school children. By and by he procured a copy of the *Topical Textbook* as a help in Bible study, and began to prepare an address on "The Bible." This was the subject of his first attempt at a Bible reading.

His method was simple, and suited to the needs of the case. He would call upon someone in the audience to read a certain text. This would give him time to collect his thoughts, and he would then say a few words or relate an anecdote to light up the text. When he found himself running dry, he would call for another text to be read, and on this he would offer a few comments in a similar fashion.

When his audiences became larger, so that he had to read the texts himself, he had to make better preparation beforehand, as there was less opportunity for impromptu comment.

Before long he received an invitation from Dr. Goodwin, pastor of the First Congregational

Church, Chicago, to repeat one of these Bible readings in his church.

"I rubbed my eyes," he said, "to see who I was!"

He had never anticipated that he would get that far in public ministry. The Bible reading he gave at Dr. Goodwin's church was on the Holy Spirit.

He next received an invitation to give a Bible reading in the Third Presbyterian Church, and by degrees his reputation spread.

He never really changed his method of making sermons, which was as follows:

Having decided to prepare an address on any topic or text (he preferred to use subjects mostly), his first step was to take a large envelope, and on the outside write the title or reference: "Heaven"— "Psalm 23"—"Backsliders"—"Let the wicked forsake"—"How To Deal with Inquirers."

Into such envelopes he crowded extracts copied from sermons and commentaries, cuttings from newspapers, original thoughts and suggestions, anecdotes and illustrations from his own experience— scraps of all kinds that had any bearing on the subject under consideration.

Whenever Mr. Moody wished to preach on a certain subject, he ran through the envelope of thoughts and clippings, and selected such points and anecdotes as he wished to use on that occasion. Weaving these into an outline, and taking sheets of note paper, he wrote out catchwords, and fastened the sheets into his Bible by means of elastic bands.

Here he began by considering objections. First: "I do not feel enough for my sins."

This objection he proposed to meet by quoting Ezekiel 33:11; so he cut that verse out of a large print Bible and pasted it onto this sheet, in order to avoid the necessity of turning up the reference.

At some later period he added, "Has not struck me," to remind him of another frequent excuse.

Second objection: "How much and long should I feel sorry for my sins?"

This he met with II Corinthians 7:9, 10. Also with the command of Isaiah 55:7: "Let the wicked forsake his way, and the unrighteous man his thoughts, and let him return unto the Lord."

"I have repented far more since I came to Christ than before," he next wrote, reminding himself of a line of thought that he was fond of pressing home—namely, that repentance and the new birth are only the beginnings of an experience during which the Christian may constantly need to repent of sin, and rely on the Saviour's help.

This method of making sermons he found gave full opportunity for impromptu inspiration, as the preacher is not bound hard and fast to a written manuscript. Many of Mr. Moody's best and most often quoted sayings were unpremeditated. He always insisted that what the church needs is "men who can think on their feet."

It avoids monotony and formality in the frequent repetition of a sermon. "People say I repeat my sermons," said Mr. Moody. "Of course I do; I am glad to do so. If you have a sermon that has been blessed of God, don't be afraid to use it again and again." He must have repeated some of his sermons hundreds, if not thousands, of times. The

Bible remains a fountain of perennial interest. Credit must be given to his method of sermon-making, which permitted a variation of outline that meant continual freshness in the substance of his address, and in the order in which his points and anecdotes were marshaled.

There are three books which he advised every Christian to procure: (1) a good substantial copy of the Bible, with large clear print; (2) a *Cruden's Concordance;* and (3) a Topical Textbook.

We have already seen how he turned to the last named when preparing for Bible readings. He always kept one at hand in his study, and also a concordance. He was a Christian five years before he heard of a concordance. A skeptic in Boston got hold of him shortly after his conversion, and young Moody tried to defend the Bible and Christianity. The skeptic made a misquotation. Moody said it wasn't in the Bible, and hunted for days and days to prove the skeptic wrong. He came later to realize that if he had had a concordance, he could have found the passage in question in a few moments.

His Bibles are among the most precious treasures. He had a large number—upward of a score—in constant use, several almost worn out; leaves loose and ragged-edged, but invaluable because of the notes and suggestions written on the margins and blank spaces.

He had a dozen "interleaved" Bibles—that is, Bibles in which every other page was left blank for notes and comments. He found that notebooks and clippings accumulated quickly, and were likely to be laid aside and never referred to again. He adopted interleaved Bibles where notes were always at hand. From these he used to give out "nuggets" at his meetings, and when friends borrowed a Bible in order to copy off the notes, they were expected to write in some nuggets before returning.

"Don't be afraid to borrow or lend Bibles," he used to say. "Some time ago a man wanted to take my Bible home to get a few things out of it; and when it came back I found this note in it:

> *Jesus only:*
>   The light of Heaven is the face of Jesus.
>   The joy of Heaven is the presence of Jesus.
>   The melody of Heaven is the name of Jesus.
>   The harmony of Heaven is the praise of Jesus.
>   The theme of Heaven is the work of Jesus.
>   The employment of Heaven is the service of Jesus.
>   The duration of Heaven is the eternity of Jesus.
>   The fullness of Heaven is Jesus Himself.

He used to say it would be worth going a thousand miles to get a good thought. With what keenness he listened to other preachers, and how his face lit up with a smile as he took out the notebook he kept in his hip-pocket for nuggets!

He was an untiring Bible student. He usually arose about daybreak in summer, in order to have two or three hours alone with his Bible and his God, while his mind was fresh, and before the activities of the day divided his attention.

Among the volumes he prized most is a large pulpit Bible that contains the following inscription:

Mr. D. L. Moody, from Mrs. C. H. Spurgeon, in tender memory of the beloved one gone home to God. This Bible has been used by my precious husband, and is now given with unfeigned pleasure to one in whose hands its blessed service will be continued and extended.

S. SPURGEON.

Westwood, London, November 20, 1892.

This is the original Bible in which C. H. Spurgeon kept track of his sermons as they were printed. By means of red ink entries in the margin, he knew at once in what volume or magazine any sermon might be found. It was not the Bible Mr. Spurgeon used daily, but Mrs. Spurgeon transcribed the inscription from that one and pasted it on the flyleaf of the copy she gave Mr. Moody. It reads as follows:

C. H. Spurgeon. 1856.
The lamp of my study.
The light is as bright as ever. 1861.
Oh, that mine eyes were more opened! 1864.
Being worn to pieces, rebound 1870. The lantern mended and the light as joyous to mine eyes as ever.

Since Mr. Spurgeon's Bible came into Mr. Moody's possession (and at the same time a complete set of his sermons) , he was in the habit of turning to it first to see if Mr. Spurgeon had preached on any text he was studying.

Chapter 7

THE CIVIL WAR PERIOD

THE OUTBREAK of the Civil War opened up another avenue of Christian activity to Mr. Moody.

He had been an abolitionist since his Boston days, and took keen interest in the progress of current events. The day Lincoln's call for soldiers was issued, he was at a Sunday-school convention at Sycamore, Illinois. Turning to a friend, K. A. Burnell, he said:

"We'll have to go, but we're here now. Let us do what we can to win a multitude of souls to Christ today."

Lincoln's visit to the North Market Hall had awakened intensest feelings of patriotism in the scholars, and seventy-five of them responded to his call. Naturally Mr. Moody's heart followed them into service. Near the southern limits of Chicago, Camp Douglas was the place where ten thousand rebel prisoners were later sent on parole. An army and navy committee was immediately organized at the YMCA. With this the Northwestern Branch of the United States Christian Commission was affiliated, after the parent organization was founded, November 16, 1861. Mr. Moody did not care to engage himself to the Christian Commission, as he feared it would curtail his liberty and embarrass him in his wider work, nor would he accept urgent invitations to become a chaplain for similar reasons.

In a letter to his mother dated November 19, 1861, he wrote:

"I think you would like to attend our meetings in the North Market Hall. They are very large and interesting. Some nights fifteen or twenty rise for prayer. . . . I am now at work among the soldiers a good deal of the time. I had a good time in Kentucky. The boys wanted to have me become their chaplain, but my friends would not let me go, so I shall remain in the city. . . . . I would like to see you all, and talk with you about my Saviour, who seems so near to me. Oh, what would life be without Christ! I sometimes get to looking down on this dark world of sin, but when I look to Jesus it makes me look up."

One of his brothers (Warren) enlisted. This fact turned his heart toward the army camps. Writing to his mother on September 13, 1862, he asked to be kept exactly informed as to Warren's movements, so that he could send him books. "I am holding meetings at the camp every night with the soldiers. A good many of them are turning from the error of their ways. Tell George and Ed [two brothers at Northfield] not to let that prayer meeting go down. Pray on. They have great reason to pray now. God seems to be waiting to have this nation call on Him. I do hope these meetings will be kept up, and that the friends of Jesus will not grow weary, and, Mother, I wish you would talk to Warren about his soul. Tell him that you will pray for him daily, and God will answer your prayers. Tell him not to play cards, for it leads to gambling, and gambling leads to Hell."

By Gospel services, prayer meetings, song services (religious and patriotic), distribution of Bibles, books and tracts, and by personal visitation, he tried to win the soldiers to Christ. He organized the professed Christians into "Bands of Brothers," who were to carry "the Banner of Christ" with them, and be loyal to each other and to the cause they professed. The Seventy-second Illinois Regiment was first called the "YMCA Regiment," the idea being to have a regiment of Ironsides, every man in the ranks a Christian. He reveled in the abundant opportunities the gathering of the troops gave him for Christian activity.

Nine times he went to the front, sometimes as a member of the Christian Commission to preach and minister to the soldiers, sometimes at the request of the Sanitary Commission or the Chicago Citizens' Committee to take supplies to the wounded after battle. He was on the ground ministering to the wounded after the battles of Fort Donelson, Pittsburgh Landing, Shiloh, and Murfreesboro, with the army at Cleveland and Chattanooga, and among the first to enter Richmond.

He was a great favorite with the soldiers, highly respected for his self-sacrificing labors. Each evening, while at the front, the boys would gather round a blazing fire and listen to his earnest appeals. It was his habit to drop into the tents and talk earnestly to the soldiers, remonstrating with those who indulged in profanity. Knowing many of the soldiers in several of the regiments, he was personally solicitous for their welfare, and prayed God to give them victory over sin, Satan, and the rebels. His voice might often be heard rising in prayer from the tents of the ungodly. While serving with the command of General O. O. Howard, who was in thorough sympathy with his efforts, his ministry was especially fruitful.

In many ways these war experiences served to prepare him for his larger work. It brought him prominently before the whole country. The Chicago noon prayer meetings became a rallying-ground, where Mr. Moody and his fellow workers met and reported on their frequent excursions to the front. People from all over the Northwest sent in requests for prayer at these meetings, on behalf of husbands, brothers, sons. Mr. Moody learned, in dealing with the dying, how dangerous it is to delay in the matter of eternal salvation, hence his faculty of prompt personal dealing with the unsaved was developed. He learned precious truths as to the comforts of the Gospel, the readiness of God to hear and answer prayer, and the value of His promise. His own faith increased. Besides, he gathered a fund of anecdotes and incidents which proved effective in after years in lighting up his sermons.

Chapter 8

FARWELL HALL ACTIVITIES

ONE OF THE TURNING POINTS in the history of the YMCA in Chicago, and indeed throughout the world, occurred that day when three young men— L. M. Beam, B. F. Jacobs, and D. L. Moody—met and signed a covenant to pray and work for a building for the Association, which at that time held meetings in rented quarters that offered only limited facilities for its work.

The board of managers of the YMCA thought, planned, and prayed for a building of their own; they did everything but act. Finally it was proposed that Mr. Moody, who had recently been successful in erecting the Illinois Street Church, should be elected president, and John V. Farwell, vice-president. But Mr. Moody was considered too radical to head the ticket, so the names were reversed. While the election was proceeding, he was out getting pledges, and before night a building was assured that should contain a hall with seating capacity of three thousand, as well as rooms for smaller meetings, and offices. It was claimed to be the first YMCA building in existence.

Cyrus McCormick, who had full confidence in Mr. Moody, subscribed ten thousand dollars, the largest money gift that had been entrusted to him up to that time.

The dedication of this building to the service of Almighty God on September 26, 1867, was a notable event in religious annals. George H. Stuart, president of the United States Christian Commission, traveled eight hundred miles to be present. The hall was filled to its utmost capacity, many visitors gathering from other towns and states. The interdenominational character of the YMCA was proved by the presence of ministers of all denominations—and this at a time when its work was only beginning, and jealous eyes were watching lest it should prove to be a rival of the churches.

Mr. Moody's speech that night recounted the goodness of God in leading them from small beginnings to their present position of influence. He advocated aggressive attack upon the strongholds of sin, saying they had been on the defensive too long. He prophesied that the work was only in its infancy.

It was intended to name the hall after Mr. Moody, in honor of his strenuous and successful efforts on its behalf; but when the proper moment came he took the platform and made a short, passionate appeal that the audience name it "Farwell Hall," in honor of the man who was chairman of the Building Committee and a liberal helper. The proposal was carried with acclamation.

He raised money at one time and another for the erection of scores of churches, missions, and Association buildings in Great Britain and America, but he disclaimed all honor for his share in the work, and always suppressed attempts to use his name.

The following January the building was burned, entailing great loss, as it was only partially insured. Mr. Moody took matters in hand so promptly, however, that the noon prayer meeting was held without break, in other quarters, and it was said he had subscriptions for a new building before the fire was out. The following year the second Farwell Hall was completed and dedicated, superior in many respects to the first. This second building followed its predecessor in the great fire of 1871, when the original covenant, referred to above, was also burned.

For two years Mr. Moody was president of the YMCA.

Chapter 9

FIRST VISIT TO ENGLAND AND THE CONTINENT IN 1867

IN 1867, THE DOCTOR suggested a sea voyage for Mrs. Moody, who had a harassing cough. As Mr. Moody had an earnest desire to hear and meet Spurgeon and Müller, it was therefore decided that they make a journey to England. They started on February 22 of that year.

At this time Mr. Moody was unknown in England, except to such friends as had visited America. Among these was Fountain J. Hartley, secretary of the London Sunday School Union, who invited him to speak at an anniversary meeting in Exeter Hall. It is customary in England for a speaker on such an occasion to be connected with a formal resolution, as its mover or seconder, in order to give him a right to the floor. Mr. Moody was therefore assigned to move a vote of thanks to the chairman of the evening who in this instance was the well-known Earl of Shaftesbury.

Toward the close of the meeting the chairman yielded his place to the vice-chairman, in order that such a resolution could be offered. The vice-chairman announced that they were glad to welcome their "American cousin, the Reverend Mr.

Moody, of Chicago," who would now "move a vote of thanks to the noble Earl" who had presided on this occasion.

This program was quite out of Mr. Moody's way of doing things. With refreshing frankness and an utter disregard for conventionalities and mere compliments, he burst upon the audience with the bold announcement:

"The chairman has made two mistakes. To begin with I'm not the 'Reverend' Mr. Moody at all. I'm plain D. L. Moody, a Sunday school worker. And then I'm not your 'American cousin.' By the grace of God I'm your brother, who is interested, with you, in our Father's work for His children.

"And now about this vote of thanks to 'the noble Earl' for being our chairman this evening. I don't see why we should thank him, any more than he should thank us. When at one time they offered to thank our Mr. Lincoln for presiding over a meeting in Illinois, he stopped it. He said he'd tried to do his duty, and they'd tried to do theirs. He thought it was an even thing all round."

That opening fairly took the breath away from the audience. Its novelty was delightful, and he carried his English hearers from that time on.

He soon found his way to the YMCA in Aldersgate Street, and his experiences of Gospel work in Chicago were told with a freshness and vigor that captivated all who heard him. The unique and original way in which he pursued his reclamatory efforts among the rough and lawless children of Chicago were described with thrilling interest.

He had an interview with Mr. Spurgeon, but

failed to induce him to make a trip to America. He also went to Bristol. "Bristol," he wrote to his mother, "is where George Müller's great orphan schools are. He has 1,150 children in his house, but never asks a man for a cent of money to support them. He calls on God, and God sends the money to him. It is wonderful to see what God can do with a man of prayer."

Before sailing from New York, a friend had advised him strongly not to miss meeting the missionary veteran, Dr. Duff, and also to see Dr. Guthrie's work at Edinburgh. Thither, therefore, he went; and while he failed in his special purpose, he had the opportunity of speaking one night in the Free Assembly Hall, and met several prominent religious leaders.

He also visited Dublin, Ireland, and met Harry Moorehouse, "the boy preacher," who introduced himself, and said he would like to come to Chicago and preach.

* * *

This incident had an important sequel, which may be told in Mr. Moody's own words, as follows:

> I looked at him. He was a beardless boy; didn't look as if he was more than seventeen; and I said to myself: "He can't preach." He wanted me to let him know what boat I was going on, as he would like to return with me. I thought he could not preach, and did not let him know. But I had not been in Chicago a great many weeks before I got a letter which said he had arrived in this country, and that he would come to Chicago and preach for me if I wanted him. I sat down and

wrote a very cold letter: "If you come west, call
on me." I thought that would be the last I should
hear of him, but soon I got another letter. He
was still in this country, and would come on if I
wanted him. I wrote again, telling him if he happened to come west to drop in on me. In the
course of a few days I got a letter stating that next
Thursday he would be in Chicago. What to do
with him I did not know. I had made up my
mind he couldn't preach. I was going to be out
of town Thursday and Friday, and I told some of
the officers of the church:

"There is a man coming here Thursday and
Friday who wants to preach. I don't know wheth-
er he can or not. You had better let him try, and
I will be back Saturday."

They said there was a good deal of interest in
the church, and they did not think they should
have him preach then; he was a stranger, and he
might do more harm than good.

"Well," I said, "you had better try him. Let
him preach two nights."

When I got back Saturday morning, I was anxious to know how he got on. The first thing I
said to my wife was:

"How is that young Irishman coming along?"
(I had met him in Dublin, and took him to be an
Irishman, but he happened to be an English-
man.) "How do the people like him?"

"They like him very much."

"Did you hear him?"

"Yes."

"Did you like him?"

"Yes, very much. He has preached two sermons
from John 3:16: 'For God so loved the world,
that he gave his only begotten Son, that whoso-

ever believeth in him should not perish, but have everlasting life'; and I think you will like him, although he preaches a little different from what you do."

"How is that?"

"Well, he tells sinners God loves them."

"Well," said I, "he is wrong."

She said: "I think you will agree with him when you hear him, because he backs up everything he says with the Word of God. You think if a man doesn't preach as you do, he is wrong."

I went down that night to church, and I noticed everyone brought his Bible.

"My friends," began Moorehouse, "if you will turn to the third chapter of John and the sixteenth verse, you will find my text."

He preached a most extraordinary sermon from that verse. He did not divide the text into "secondly" and "thirdly" and "fourthly"—he just took it as a whole, and then went through the Bible, from Genesis to Revelation, to prove that in all ages God loved the world; that He sent prophets and patriarchs and holy men to warn them, and last of all sent His Son. After they murdered Him, He sent the Holy Ghost.

I never knew up to that time that God loved us so much. This heart of mine began to thaw out, and I could not keep back the tears. It was like news from a far country. I just drank it in.

The next night there was a great crowd, for the people like to hear that God loves them. He said: "My friends, if you will turn in your Bible to the third chapter of John and the sixteenth verse, you will find my text." He preached another extraordinary sermon from that wonderful verse, and he went on proving God's love again, from Genesis to Revelation. He could turn to almost any part of the Bible, and prove it. I thought that sermon was better than the other one; he struck a higher chord. It was sweet to my soul to hear it.

The next night—it is pretty hard to get out a crowd in Chicago on Monday night, but they came. Women left their washing, or if they washed, they came, and brought their Bibles; and he said again: "My friends, if you will turn to the sixteenth verse of the third chapter of John, you will find my text"; and again he followed it out to prove that God loves us. He just beat it down into our hearts, and I have never doubted it since.

I used to preach that God was behind the sinner with a double-edged sword, ready to hew him down. I have got done with that. I preach now that God is behind the sinner with love and he is running away from the God of love.

Tuesday night came, and we thought surely he had exhausted that text, and that he would take another, but he preached the sixth sermon from that wonderful text. "God so loved the world, that he gave his only begotten Son, that whosoever believeth in him should not perish, but have"—not going to have when you die, but have it right here, now—"eternal life." Although many years have rolled away, his hearers never have forgotten it.

The seventh night came, and he went into the pulpit. Every eye was upon him. All were anxious to know what he was going to preach about. He said: "My friends, I have been hunting all day for a new text, but I cannot find one as good as the old one; so we will go back to the third chapter of John and the sixteenth verse," and he preached the seventh sermon from that wonderful text. I remember the closing up of that sermon. Said he: "My friends, for a whole week I have been trying to tell you how much God loves you, but I cannot do it with this poor stammering tongue. If I could borrow Jacob's ladder, and climb up into Heaven, and ask Gabriel, who stands in the presence of the Almighty, if he could tell me how much love the Father has for the world, all he could say would be: 'God so loved the world, that he gave his only begotten Son, that whosoever believeth in him should not perish, but have eternal life.' "

It was a revelation to Mr. Moody of the inexhaustibility of Scripture such as he had never dreamed of. From that time he became a more diligent student of the Bible. He asked Moorehouse how to study, and invited friends to his Chicago home for the first "Bible readings" that were held in America.

*   *   *

The only other place of special interest that Mr. Moody visited on this trip was Paris. He went there with his wife for a week in order to avoid the trying English climate. He preached a few times with the help of interpreters. The Paris Exposition was then in progress.

He left a permanent impress upon English religious life by establishing a noon prayer meeting at the Aldersgate Street YMCA similar to the Chicago noon prayer meeing. "I have sent you an account of the daily noon prayer meeting I have at last got started here," he wrote his mother. "It is a great success, and they are starting them in different parts of the city. I am in hopes great good will come from it. They are also starting them in different parts of the kingdom."

Chapter 10

HOW MOODY AND SANKEY FIRST CAME TOGETHER

MR. MOODY'S NAME is, throughout the world, associated with that of Ira D. Sankey more than any other of his fellow laborers in the Gospel.

They met for the first time in the year 1870, at the International Convention of the Young Men's Christian Association, held in Indianapolis, Indiana.

They had heard of each other, but had never met. Mr. Sankey was already known for his ability to win souls by his singing of hymns, but neither figured very prominently as leaders of the exercises at the convention.

At that time Mr. Sankey was a government officer in New Castle, Pennsylvania, holding a commission in the Internal Revenue service. He was thirty years old, of English and Scotch-Irish stock, born at Edinburgh, Lawrence County, Pennsylvania, on August 28, 1840. He was a member of the Methodist Episcopal Church, but his religious work had been conducted only during leisure hours, and from an early age had been in the direction of singing.

He had heard enough of Mr. Moody to become

curious to see him and hear him talk. When he
went to the Indianapolis convention he looked for
the young man from Chicago.

Their first meeting did not occur until a day or
so after their arrival, and then only under rather
novel circumstances.

It was announced that "Mr. Moody from Chicago" would conduct a prayer meeting on Sunday
morning at six o'clock, in a Baptist church some
distance away from the Academy of Music, the convention site. Notwithstanding the early hour, Mr.
Sankey determined to take advantage of the opportunity to see and hear the man.

The distance to the church was much greater
than he had anticipated, so the service was half
through when he arrived and took a seat near the
door.

At the conclusion of a lengthy prayer, a friend,
Rev. Robert McMillen, urged Mr. Sankey to start
right in with a hymn, as there seemed to be no one
in charge of the singing. Without waiting for further invitation, Mr. Sankey rose and sang:

> There is a fountain filled with blood,
>   Drawn from Immanuel's veins;
> And sinners plunged beneath that flood
>   Lose all their guilty stains.

The congregation joined in heartily.

When the meeting closed, Mr. McMillen asked
Mr. Sankey to step forward, and he would intro-
duce him to Mr. Moody.

As he drew near, Mr. Moody, recognizing the

one who had led the singing, took his hand, and said:

"Where are you from?"

"Pennsylvania," replied Mr. Sankey.

"Married?"

"Yes. I have a wife and two children."

"What do you do for a living when you are at home?"

"I am in the government service."

All this time Mr. Moody had been holding Mr. Sankey's hand. Looking into his face with his keen eyes, he said:

"Well, you'll have to give up business."

Mr. Sankey was at a loss to understand just what Mr. Moody meant by telling him he would have to give up what was to him a good position, and one affording a comfortable living. He was so taken aback for a few seconds that he could make no reply. Mr. Moody explained:

"You'll have to give up your government position, and come with me. You are the man I have been looking for for the last eight years. I want you to come and help me in my work in Chicago."

Mr. Sankey had by this time partly recovered from his surprise, but the thought of giving up a good position for an uncertainty was too much, and he begged for time in which to consider the matter. Mr. Moody asked him if he would pray over the question, and out of politeness he said he would.

That was Sunday. All that day and night Mr. Sankey thought over Mr. Moody's words, but the next morning found him still inclined to stick to the government position, with his salary assured every month.

Just at a moment when he was inclined to waver a card was brought to him. It was from Mr. Moody, asking him to meet him that evening at six o'clock at a certain street corner to sing.

Mr. Sankey wrote an acceptance upon the back of the card, and returned it to Mr. Moody, saying he would be there. Together with a few friends he went to the appointed place at the hour named. In a few moments Mr. Moody came along.

Without stopping, he walked into a store and asked for the use of a large store box for a pulpit. Permission being given, he rolled the box out to the street corner, and climbing upon it, asked Mr. Sankey to sing a hymn.

After one or two hymns had been sung, Mr. Moody commenced to preach. The workingmen were just on their way home from the mills and factories, and in a short time a large crowd had gathered. Mr. Sankey says that Mr. Moody preached that evening from that box as he had never heard anyone preach before.

The crowd stood spellbound as the words flowed from his lips with wonderful force and rapidity. After he had talked for about fifteen minutes, he leaped down from the box, announced that he was going to hold a meeting at the Academy of Music, and invited the crowd to accompany him there. Mr. Sankey and his friends marched down the street four abreast, singing "Shall We Gather at the River?"

It took but a few minutes to pack the lower floor of the Academy of Music. Mr. Moody saw that the men in their working clothes were seated before he ascended the platform to speak.

His second address was as captivating as the one delivered on the street corner, and it was not until the delegates had arrived for the evening session of the convention that the meeting was brought to a close.

Mr. Sankey was still undecided when Mr. Moody again brought up the question of their becoming a team. However, the impression made on his mind by those two services was so great that after a period of several months he accepted an invitation to spend a week with Mr. Moody in Chicago. Before that week was over he had sent his commission to the Secretary of the Treasury.

From that time to the day of Mr. Moody's death they continued their labors in unbroken harmony and accord.

Mr. Moody's opinion as to the value of singing in religious services was very decided. He said:

"I feel sure the great majority of people do like singing, and I purpose to make it a prominent feature of all my services. It helps to build up your audience—even if you do preach a dry sermon. If you have singing that reaches the heart, it will fill the church."

He used to say that there is more said in the Bible about praise than about prayer, and that music and song not only accompanied all Scripture revivals, but were essential in deepening spiritual life. "We owe some of our best hymns to seasons

like those, when in the family and church, in the
factory and street, the great truths of the Gospel
are heard in song. Singing does at least as much as
preaching to impress the Word of God upon people's minds. During the forty years since God first
called me, the importance of praise expressed in
song has grown upon me." His constant effort was
to promote good, lively singing in the church, also
in the home.

Chapter 11

THE CHICAGO FIRE, AND AFTER

THE YEAR 1871 was critical in Mr. Moody's career. He realized more and more how little he was fitted by personal acquirements for his work. An intense hunger and thirst for spiritual power were aroused in him by the action of three holy women, who used to attend his meetings and sit on the front seat. He could see by the expression on their faces that they were praying. At the close of services they would say to him:

"We have been praying for you."

"Why don't you pray for the people?" he would ask.

"Because you need the power of the Spirit," they said.

"I need the power! Why," said Mr. Moody, speaking of it in after years, "I thought I had power. I had the largest congregations in Chicago, and there were many conversions. I was in a sense satisfied. But right along, those three godly women kept praying for me, and their earnest talk about anointing for special service set me to thinking. I asked them to come and talk with me, and we got down on our knees. They poured out their hearts that I might receive the filling of the Holy Spirit. There came a great hunger into my soul. I did not know what it was. I began to cry as I never did before. The hunger increased. I really felt that I did not want to live any longer if I could not have this power for service."

While he was in this mental and spiritual condition, Chicago was laid in ashes. The great fire commenced on October 8, 1871, and swept out of existence both Farwell Hall and Illinois Street Church. He had been preaching a series of sermons on the life of Christ in Farwell Hall for five Sunday nights. He took the Saviour from the cradle and followed Him up to the judgment hall. That night Mr. Moody made what he considered the greatest blunder he ever made in his life. The courthouse bell was sounding an alarm of fire, but he paid no attention to it. They were accustomed to hear the fire-bell often, and it did not disturb them.

He finished his sermon upon "What shall I do with Jesus?" and said to the audience:

"Now, I want you to take the question with you and think it over, and next Sunday I want you to come back and tell me what you are going to do with Him."

"What a mistake!" he said afterward; "it seems as if Satan was in my mind when I said it. Since then I have never dared to give an audience a week to think of their salvation. If they were lost, they might rise up in judgment against me.

"I remember Mr. Sankey singing, and how his voice rang when he came to that pleading verse:

> Today the Saviour calls,
>   For refuge fly!
> The storm of Justice falls,
>   And death is nigh!

After the meeting, as Mr. Moody went homeward, he saw the glare of flames, and knew it meant ruin to Chicago. About one o'clock Farwell Hall was burned. Soon his church went down. Everything was scattered. About midnight the fierceness of the fire seemed to be waning. They thought the fire department would gain the upper hand, as they had done the night before. The family retired, but within an hour a loud call was made to all the residents of their street to hasten their escape. The fire had crossed the river, and was rapidly advancing.

It was too late to think of saving much more than could be carried. A neighbor took Mr. Moody's two children in his already crowded carriage, and made his escape north. A few articles of silver and some valued tokens of friendships were hastily placed in a baby-cart. But there was one article Mrs. Moody's heart was set upon saving. This was a portrait in oil of her husband by the artist Healy, that hung on the wall of their parlor. It was a gift from the artist, presented to Mrs. Moody after the return from the first trip to Europe in 1867, when a free lease of this home, completely furnished, was presented to Mr. Moody by his Chicago friends. This portrait Mrs. Moody prized above anything the home contained.

A stranger who entered the house assisted in taking it from the wall. Calling Mr. Moody, his wife urged him to save it for her.

No entreaty could prevail on him, but the canvas was hastily knocked out of the heavy gold frame. and carried off by Mrs. Moody herself.

A black eye and a bruised face was part of the price paid for this effort. Once on the street it was a constant struggle between the bearer of the panel and the terrific wind that was blowing. Love won, but only after a continuous battle.

When they were safe, he said:

"Wouldn't it have been amusing for me to take my own picture! Suppose I was met on the street by friends in the same plight as ourselves, and they said: 'Hello, Moody, glad you have escaped; what's that you have saved and cling to so affectionately?'— wouldn't it have sounded fine to reply, 'Oh, I've got my own picture'?"

The portrait was hung on the wall of the North-field home, bringing to mind that night of fiery ordeal that tried many a man's soul.

As soon as his wife and family were safe with friends, Mr. Moody devoted himself to relief work. Before long he left for the East to raise money for the homeless, and also for a new church. George H. Stuart and John Wanamaker, of Philadelphia, and other friends raised three thousand dollars, and a temporary building, seventy-five by one hundred feet, was immediately erected on a lot not far from the site of the former church. On December 24, 1871, just two months and fifteen days after the fire, this building, known as the North Side Tabernacle, was dedicated.

But that eastern visit was productive of greater blessing in Mr. Moody's life. The hunger for more spiritual power was still upon him. The fire did not dismiss the yearning. "My heart was not in the work for begging," he said. "I could not appeal. I was crying all the time that God would fill me with His Spirit. Well, one day, in the city of New York—ah, what a day!—I cannot describe it, I seldom refer to it, it is almost too sacred an experience to name—Paul had an experience of which he never spoke for fourteen years—I can only say God revealed Himself to me, and I had such an experience of His love that I had to ask Him to stay His hand. I went to preaching again. The sermons were not different; I did not present any new truths; and yet hundreds were converted. I would not now be placed back where I was before that blessed experience if you should give me all the world; it would be as the small dust of the balance."

When he returned to Chicago, his mission work at the new tabernacle went forward successfully. Revival fires were kindled anew and blazed long and bright.

Within a year steps were taken to erect a permanent building. The lot on Chicago Avenue and LaSalle was secured. Contributions came in from all quarters, thousands of Sunday school children contributing five cents each to buy bricks. For two years the basement was roofed over temporarily, and used for meetings. Finally, as a subsequent chapter will explain, means were provided for the completion of the structure, which became known as the Chicago Avenue Church, or Moody's Church.

Chapter 12

SECOND VISIT TO ENGLAND, 1872

WHILE THE AUDIENCES at the North Side Tabernacle were large and the meetings fruitful in results, it was impossible for Mr. Moody to do any visitation work, as there were no homes within reach. The fire had laid the city in ashes for a large area surrounding the tabernacle. Where the people came from to attend the meetings was a mystery. Such as built shanties among the ruins were constantly moving.

Finding, therefore, that he could be spared from Chicago, and desiring to learn more of the Bible at the feet of English Bible students, Mr. Moody determined to cross the sea again. He did in June, 1872.

This visit demands special consideration on account of one incident.

He was determined not to get into work if he could help it; but one day he went into the Old Bailey prayer meeting, and at the close of the service the Rev. Mr. Lessey, pastor of a church in the north of London, asked him to preach the next Sunday. Mr. Moody consented.

The place seemed very dead and cold at the morning service. The people did not appear to be

very much interested. It seemed to him as if he had
been beating the air.

The next service was at half-past six in the evening. While he was preaching, it seemed as if the
atmosphere was charged with the Spirit of God.
There came a hush from Heaven upon the people,
which showed that God was searching hearts. He
had not been much in prayer that day, and could
not understand it.

When he had finished preaching, he asked all
who would like to become Christians to rise, so
that he might pray for them. They rose by hundreds; it seemed as if the whole audience was getting up.

Mr. Moody said to himself: "These people did
not understand me. They did not know what I
meant when I asked them to rise."

He had never seen so many rise in America, and
did not know what to make of it.

"Now," he said, "all of you that want to become
Christians just step into the inquiry room."

They went in and crowded the room so that they
had to take in extra chairs to seat them all. The
minister was surprised, and so was Mr. Moody.
Neither had expected such a blessing. They had
not faith to believe that God can save by hundreds
and thousands as well as by ones and twos.

When Mr. Moody again asked those who really
wanted to become Christians to rise, up rose the
whole audience. What to do he did not know, so
he told all who were really in earnest to meet the
pastor there the next night.

Next day he went over to Dublin. On Tuesday

morning he got a dispatch urging him to return, saying that there were more inquirers on Monday than on Sunday. He went back and held meetings for ten days. Four hundred were taken into that church.

After some time the secret of this marvelous manifestation of the Spirit's working was revealed. There were two sisters who belonged to that church. One was strong, the other was bedridden. One day, as the sick woman was bemoaning her condition, the thought came that she could pray. She began to pray God to revive the church of which she was a member. Day and night her prayer went up to God, but the church remained cold and dead.

Before long she read in a paper an account of some meetings Mr. Moody had held in America, and, though she did not know him, she began to pray God to send him to her church.

Her sister came home that Sunday after he had preached, and said:

"Well, who do you think preached this morning?"

She guessed the names of a good many with whom her pastor was in the habit of exchanging.

Finally her sister said, "It was Mr. Moody, from America."

The bedridden saint turned pale, and said:

"I know what that means. God has heard my prayer."

She spent that afternoon in fasting and prayer, and in the evening the answer came from Heaven. Mr. Moody believed that that revival brought him back to England the next year. As a result of it, he

received invitations from Rev. William Penne-
father, rector of St. Jude's, Mildmay Park, London,
and a Mr. Bainbridge, a prominent Methodist lay-
man of Newcastle-on-Tyne, to hold meetings. He
had not come prepared for a long stay, so returned
to America after three months and rejoined his
family. He was urgently invited, however, to return to England next year.

Chapter 13

GREAT ENGLISH CAMPAIGN WITH MR. SANKEY, 1873-75

Mr. Moody decided to accept the invitation that had been pressed upon him, and waited for the funds they promised to send him for the expense of the ocean voyage. He arranged with Mr. Sankey, who was at that time chorister of his church and Sunday school, to accompany him.

Steamship passage was engaged for both families, but weeks went by and the promised funds did not arrive. He could not understand it. Finally, believing that God's leading was distinctly toward England, he was obliged to go to a friend with whom he had just deposited about four hundred and fifty dollars to invest during his absence, and take back the money. Another friend, quite unconscious of the real situation, handed him a check for five hundred dollars the day before he left Chicago. The greater portion of these two sums was expended in paying for ocean passage for the party.

They arrived at Queenstown in due time. There Mr. Moody received word that explained the nonreceipt of the promised money. The two cordial and devoted Christian friends on whom he was relying for moral and financial support had both died.

After reading the letter, Mr. Moody turned to Mr. Sankey and said:

"God seems to have closed the door. We will not open any ourselves. If He opens the door we will go in; otherwise we will return at once to America."

On landing at Liverpool, June 17, 1873, they went directly to the Northwestern Hotel. Three gentlemen, who had noticed their names in the list of arrivals, called upon them at the hotel. During the evening Mr. Moody discovered in one of his pockets an unopened letter which he had received, just before leaving New York, from the secretary of the YMCA at York, England, saying that he hoped if he ever came to England he would come and speak at their Association.

Mr. Moody at once remarked: "This door is only ajar, but we will consider the letter as God's hand leading to York, and we will go there."

After spending one night at Liverpool, Mr. Moody, with his wife and children, took the train for London. Mr. Sankey and his wife went to Manchester to the home of the one man that he knew in England—Harry Moorehouse. Three days later thy met again at York and commenced to hold meetings.

The ministers at first were inclined to look upon the newcomers with suspicion and disfavor, and consequently held aloof. The attendance was small to begin with. Gradually the meetings grew in interest, the ministers co-operated, the hymns took hold of the people, and both preaching and singing became the subject of public conversation throughout the community. The preaching was for believers rather than for the unconverted.

"Yes, thank God, I know Mr. Moody," wrote Rev. F. B. Meyer, of Christ Church, London; "I have known him ever since a memorable Monday morning in 1873. I can now see him standing up to lead the first noon prayer meeting in a small ill-lit room in Coney Street, York, little realizing that it was the seed-germ of a mighty harvest, and that a movement was beginning that would culminate in a few months in Free Assembly Hall, Edinburgh, and ultimately in the Agricultural Hall and the Royal Opera-house, London. It was the birth-time of new conceptions of ministry, new methods of work, new inspirations and hopes."

After five weeks of meetings in York, resulting in the professed conversion of several hundred people, they went to the seaport town of Sunderland. Here their meetings were largely attended. A better spirit was evident, and much larger numbers professed conversion. The chapel in which their first meetings were held soon became too small, necessitating the use of one of the largest halls in the north of England. The town had been placarded, in advance of their coming, with posters that read:

> Moody will preach the Gospel
> Sankey will sing the Gospel

—thus giving birth to the latter expression.

After six weeks spent in Sunderland and outlying districts, they were invited to Newcastle-on-Tyne.

They had now gained the sympathy of nearly all the ministers of all denominations except those of the Established Church, who, learning that they were both unordained men, refused in any way to co-operate. After a few weeks of very successful meetings, the editor of the *Newcastle Chronicle*, a Mr. Cowan, then a member of Parliament for that district, wrote about the meetings in his paper, speaking of them as a "wonderful religious phenomenon." On the whole, it was a friendly review and criticism of the work.

It was very unusual then for such a prominent secular paper to discuss religious matters, and Mr. Cowan's article created a profound impression throughout England. Invitations to hold services began to pour in.

The fame of the Newcastle revival reached Edinburgh, and ministers and laymen went to investigate. The result was an invitation from a large and representative committee to hold meetings in that city. They accepted, and the most interesting and wonderful meetings they had yet held took place.

Special preparatory prayer meetings had been organized. Everything was done to insure success. But there was much prejudice and criticism to overcome. Mr. Sankey's singing was contrary to Scottish ideas. His organ was called a "kist fu' o' whistles," and was regarded as an abomination. Mr. Moody's fiery speech and actions stood out in peculiar contrast with the staid demeanor and solemn spirit of the ordinary Scottish divine. But his simple and scriptural style of preaching soon won them. The interest was intense from the first, and the crowds enormous. No one building could accommodate the people. Three or four overflow meetings were held at the same time. The newspapers gave ample reports of the meetings, and soon the news of the revival was telegraphed all over the country.

There was a solemn stillness in the meetings, and a complete absence of emotional excitement.

All classes of society were influenced. Dr. Horatius Bonar declared his belief that there was scarcely a Christian household in the whole city in which one or more persons had not been converted. People came in from miles around to attend the meetings, or to get someone to come to their town or hamlet and tell of the wonderful work, thus spreading the fires throughout the land. It was while organizing services for students there that Mr. Moody first met Henry Drummond, himself a student. Recognizing his ability, Mr. Moody attached him getting him to devote the next year or two to work among young men.

After spending three months in Edinburgh, the evangelists went to Dundee, and then for a four months' campaign to Glasgow. "The career of these men has been like the rolling of a snowball," wrote the minister who had invited them to Sunderland; "it gathers as it goes; at first a handful, then a hill." One of the closing meetings at Glasgow was for converts, of whom thirty-five hundred were admitted by ticket. So great was the crowd on the last Sunday evening—estimated at fifty thousand—that Mr. Moody did not go inside the Kibble Crystal Palace, where the meeting was advertised to be held. He preached to the multitude in the open air, standing on the box of a carriage. Mr. Sankey conducted the meeting in the palace.

Similar scenes of revival interest followed as the evangelists visited other towns as far north as John o' Groats (northeast end of Scotland). Scotland was stirred to its depths in a degree never known before. Mr. Moody visited that country two or three times after that, with Mr. Sankey, and always with an enthusiastic welcome, with good spiritual results. Well might Lord Overtoun telegraph on the occasion of Mr. Moody's death:

"All Scotland mourns."

In September, 1874, Messrs. Moody and Sankey began meetings in Belfast, Ireland. That first Sunday, it is estimated that four times as many people gathered as could get into the building. Other centers were visited in Ireland, the tour culminating in great meetings in the Exhibition Palace in Dublin. The evangelists had made almost as deep an impression upon Ireland as upon Scotland.

Returning to England, they visited Manchester, Sheffield, Birmingham, Liverpool, and other towns, with the usual demonstrations of the Spirit and of power. Finally, on March 9, 1875, they entered upon their great London campaign, which lasted until July 12.

The immense size and population of London made it necessary to strike successively at different points so as to reach the whole city. The city and suburbs were divided into four quarters, for each of which a secretary was appointed. Local committees were also formed, subordinate to the central committee. The enthusiasm was intense. Greater crowds than ever attended. The Agricultural Hall, North London, was constantly overcrowded, although the capacity was variously estimated from fifteen to twenty thousand. The Royal Opera house, with seating capacity of five thousand, could have been filled three or four times over. The daily papers gave extended reports of the meetings. Penny editions of *Sacred Songs and Solos* were sold in the streets. Not only was London itself stirred, but the revival became a world wonder.

At this time Mr. Moody was only thirty-eight years old. Nobody was more surprised than he at the magnitude of the work initiated in York under such unpromising conditions two years before. From a little mission among the street urchins of Chicago, he had been led of God to make perhaps the deepest and most far-reaching religious impression that had as yet been made upon Great Britain and Ireland, and through these upon the whole English-speaking world.

Through it all he remained perfectly humble before God. "I am glad you have the papers," he once wrote to his mother; "it will be as good as a letter from me—in face, better, for I would not like to have to write so much about myself."

Dr. R. W. Dale, one of the leading Nonconformists of England, watched him for three or four days after he went to Birmingham, at different kinds of meetings, trying to discover the secret of his power. Then he told him that the work was most plainly of God, for he could see no relation between him personally and the work he was doing.

Mr. Moody laughed cheerily, and said he would be very sorry if it were otherwise.

Dr. Dale had a profound respect for Mr. Moody and considered that he had a right to preach the Gospel, "because," he said, "he could never speak of a lost soul without tears of Christly compassion in his eyes."

Some of the direct results of the English tour may be summarized as follows: Thousands of the unsaved and thousands of the backslidden Christians were led into closer communion with God. A spirit of evangelism was awakened, and has never died down. A large number of city missions and other active aggressive organizations were established. Denominational differences were buried to a remarkable degree. Clergymen of all denominations were drawn into co-operation on a common platform, the salvation of the lost. Bibles were reopened, and Bible study received a wonderful impetus. Long-standing prejudices were swept away. New life was infused into all methods of Christian activity. No attempt was made to proselyte, and converts were passed to existing churches for nurture and admonition in the Lord. Singing received due recognition in the worship of God. Lord Shaftesbury once said that if Mr. Sankey had done no more than teach the people to sing the hymn "Hold the Fort," he had conferred an inestimable benefit on the British Empire.

The *New York Tribune* commented editorially on the work in England as follows:

"There can be but one opinion as to the sincerity

of Messrs. Moody and Sankey. They are not money-makers, they are not charlatans. Decorous, conservative England, which reprobated both their work and the manner of it, held them in the full blaze of scrutiny for months, and could not detect in them a single motive which was not pure."

After spending a few weeks with friends in Wales, speaking occasionally, Mr. Moody preached a farewell sermon in Liverpool on August 3, 1875, and sailed for America the following day.

Chapter 14

BIRTH OF THE *MOODY AND SANKEY HYMNBOOKS*, 1873

ANOTHER ILLUSTRATION of Mr. Moody's persistence and faith was the birth and growth of the *Moody and Sankey Hymnbooks*. The great mission these books have had, not alone in singing their way with Gospel gladness into the hearts of millions, but also in singing the erection of great institutions of education and Biblical training, is one of the romances of religion and commerce.

When Mr. Moody and Mr. Sankey reached England, they found hymns in the churches different from what they had been used to, and inappropriate for their purpose. A book of their own hymns was imperative.

No publisher could be found, however, to undertake the risk of publication, as an American hymnbook previously issued had not fulfilled expectations. Standing absolutely alone, Mr. Moody was obliged to print one at his own risk and expense. He invested all the money he had left (about one hundred dollars) in a sixteen-page pamphlet of words and music, compiled by Mr. Sankey. It sold at 12 cents each. This was followed by a "words only" edition that sold at one penny (two cents) per copy.

The supply was quickly exhausted. A publisher was now found who agreed to pay a liberal royalty. This arrangement was accepted by Mr. Moody, with the thought that it might in part pay expenses for which he had obligated himself personally. So great was the growing interest that little attention was paid to the matter of royalties, which were left to accumulate. In fact, it soon became a problem as to what should be done with the sum.

At the close of the London campaign and shortly before Messrs. Moody and Sankey were to return home, the publisher's statement showed that the sum standing to their credit on this royalty account was no less than thirty-five thousand dollars. They sent word to the London committee that this amount was at their disposal, to be used for Christian work as they should direct, as they would not take a cent of the money for themselves. The committee refused to accept the fund, asserting that it belonged to them personally, and they did not propose to have them pay this large sum for the privilege of preaching.

A peculiar case—money going begging for want of a receiver!

One of the officers of the Chicago Avenue Church, Chicago, who happened to be in London at the time, hearing of this predicament, suggested to the committee that the sum be forwarded to Chicago to complete the building of that church. Owing to the panic of 1873-74, pledges made for the erection of this building had become worthless.

Work was stopped when only the first (or lecture room) story was built. A temporary roof covered this, and services had been held for two years.

The suggestion was adopted, the money paid over, and Moody's Church was completed.

So successful was the sale of succeeding hymn-books that the amount realized in royalties in America doubtless exceeded a million dollars; but not one cent of it ever found its way into the pockets of either Mr. Moody or Mr. Sankey. It has all been administered by trustees for the benefit of YMCA's, churches, and (of late years) Mr. Moody's schools at Northfield.

Chapter 15

RETURN TO AMERICA, AND THE GREAT MEETINGS IN THE SEVENTIES

IT IS BEYOND THE TRUTH to say, as some have said, that Great Britain "discovered" D. L. Moody. He was a widely known and widely honored Christian worker when he went abroad upon that momentous third visit. But it undoubtedly is true that he returned to America with his fame greatly enhanced. The display of his powers, both natural and bestowed, upon a scene so conspicuous, and the magnitude of the results achieved, profoundly impressed the whole Christian world. Indeed, from that time can be dated his world-wide fame.

Naturally, his own countrymen followed his course through the three kingdoms most closely, and with deepest interest. The newspaper stories of the unprecedented meetings in London, Liverpool, Birmingham, Manchester, Glasgow, Belfast, and Dublin spread through the United States both the desire for and faith in a great revival whenever he should return. That expectation of blessing, as is well known to students of the history of revivals, creates the atmosphere favorable to the new birth.

Months before the close of the work in England, calls for his labors had been pouring in. With his unfailing strategic insight he made his choice.

"Cities," he said, "are the centers of influence. Water runs downhill, and the highest hills in America are the great cities. If we can stir them we shall stir the whole country."

So he began that series of meetings of unequaled numbers, power, and fruitage in the religious history of this country.

Into New York, Philadelphia, Baltimore, St. Louis, Cincinnati, Chicago, Boston, and later in the lesser great cities, he carried the Gospel fire. Invariably he rallied about him the strongest laymen in the community. Men of affairs gave not only of their means to the necessary expenses of the work, but gave themselves as well. They felt of kin to this strong dominant personality, and gladly followed his leadership.

To the very end of his life he retained the unbounded confidence of men of affairs. At a dinner in New York not a year before his death, a guest said to a great railway magnate who was present:

"How is it that while you and other like men are all but inaccessible, fenced in by closed doors and polite but immovable private secretaries, D. L. Moody sees you at any time?"

"He is one of us," was the reply.

In this great series of meetings Mr. Moody's gifts were in full exercise. His methods combined the siege and the assault. Sometimes, as in Baltimore and St. Louis, he spent months in a place, studying the situation with unfailing sagacity, covering the

entire city with meetings in which he utilized the
ministers and lay workers, and often, especially toward the end, calling to his aid brother evangelists
and singers from far and near. His objects were not
only immediate results in conversion, though this,
needless to say, held the first place, but also the permanent quickening of the life of the churches, and
especially the promotion of Bible study.

He usually gave the afternoon meetings to Bible
readings, and no one who heard them will ever forget the impression of those fresh, original, and deeply spiritual expositions. But the meetings themselves were, after all, the most marvelous of all the
manifestations of power.

No church or hall could seat the thousands who
flocked to hear. In New York, the immense building known as the Hippodrome was utilized. Built
originally for a railway station, and subsequently
remodeled and filled with rising tiers of benches by
P. T. Barnum for his circus, it was admirably
adapted for such meetings. Varying in minor detail in different places, the meetings were in essen-
tials very much alike. The following interesting de-
scription, taken (by permission) from an article
in the *Ladies' Home Journal* by Nathaniel P. Bab-
cock, an eyewitness of the scenes in the Hippodrome, which he describes, may serve to give a
truthful idea of Mr. Moody's work in the seventies:

> "To the Hippodrome!" was the cry of the Prot-
> estant religious world of New York during the
> early months of the year 1876. Twenty-one years
> ago, and yet the strangeness of those days, when
> over the great metropolis hung an atmosphere

charged with the electricity of religious zeal, is fresh in my memory. "To the Hippodrome!" The words were uttered from the pulpits of scores of churches—first as advice, then as a command—by ministers to congregations. "To the Hippodrome!" You heard the phrase in the streetcars, in the hotels, sometimes upon the busy avenues. On early morning trains, steaming in from suburban points, you saw women by hundreds, with luncheons in baskets, drawn to the city, not by the spring millinery of the stores, but by that shibboleth which echoed in myriad Christian hearts, "To the Hippodrome!"

Moody and Sankey, aided by a multitude of local clergymen and bands of volunteer Christian workers, had undertaken the task of setting New York on fire with enthusiasm for the cause of Christ. How great was the measure of their success may be judged by the fact that there were days between February 7, the beginning of the revival, and April 19, its close, when as many as sixty thousand persons found their way into the presence of the evangelists—one meeting following another from noon till quite late in the evening, with almost constantly assembling audiences of seven or eight thousand at each. A monster stage or platform in the main room was built to hold a choir of six hundred voices, and still leave room for at least four hundred visiting clergymen or distinguished guests. Partitioned off at the extreme outer edge of this huge platform was the box—it could scarcely be called a pulpit—from which the exhorter was to speak. The railing needed to be strong which fenced the front of this preacher's stand, for there were times, when the upheaving of the consciences of men began and the great evangelist with earnest eyes looked into the agonized faces of the multitude before him, and his strong frame bent heavily against the barrier, his arms stretched forth as though to take the whole wide world of suffering sinners in a comforting embrace.

This is how Mr. Moody looked, when to an eager, earnest, expectant audience he appeared through that small door at the back of the stage in the Hippodrome: a sturdy figure in a tightly fitting frock coat; a well-shaped head made to look smaller than its actual size because of the broadness of the man's shoulders and the shortness of the neck on which it was poised; a much bearded face, the black hair not only hanging down over his chest, but growing thickly up each cheek; a forehead seemingly low by reason of its projection beyond the line of the nose; keen eyes, with wrinkles running from their outer corners over ruddy cheeks, and a heavy black mustache hiding the mouth. In his hands, as he came for the first time into the presence of this mighty metropolitan audience, Mr. Moody carried a Bible. His fingers were interlaced about it, but as he passed through the narrow lane between the choir and the platform guests and reached the front of the stage, he shifted the Book and lifted his right hand, palm downward, toward the vast audience. It was the signal for silence, and was heeded by everyone.

When in obedience to Mr. Moody's signal the music ceased and the audience became entirely attentive, the evangelist said:

"Let us open the meeting by silent prayer."

These were the first words uttered by this remarkable man in his work in the chief city of

America in that religious revival the effects of which spread from end to end of the American continent. As he spoke he bowed his head on the railing at the platform's edge. Then among all that vast concourse heads were reverently bent, and absolute silence prevailed.

How long this mute prayer continued I do not know. What is vividly before me is the singular commotion which followed at its close when Mr. Moody gave out the opening hymn. In all that assembly there were but few who were unprovided with hymnals, for from the date of the opening service in Brooklyn, on October 24, the Moody and Sankey Songbook had become universally popular. And now, when the command was given to "join in singing" one of those inspiring melodies, the page number of which was announced by the evangelist, ten thousand hands began to turn the leaves of these books, making a rustling noise not unlike the wind in the trees before a storm. Meanwhile, Mr. Sankey seated himself at a small organ near the front of the platform, and assumed the direction of the music.

. . . .

Down from the pulpit with outstretched hands came Mr. Moody, and as he passed through the aisles here and there, persons arose and with bowed heads walked away in the direction of doors that led to the apartments known as "inquiry rooms." Beyond these doors we may not follow them. I know that earnest men and women waited in those rooms to receive all whose agonized consciences led them there. I know that they knelt in prayer, and that words of love and sympathy were whispered in their ears, and

I remember to have seen men come forth with countenances radiant; but of the personal experiences of converted sinners we are not speaking. It is the wonderful scene of a concourse stirred by something deeper than worldly enthusiasm, deeper than brotherly love, deeper than patriotism, that we are endeavoring to recall.

. . . .

Three meetings a day—sometimes, though not often, five—is the work these evangelists have laid out for themselves. In the afternoon of many days women only are admitted to the Hippodrome. They pack it solidly from the floor to the topmost seats, till their plumes brush the rafters. "Pray for my husband!" "Pray for my son!" "Pray for my brother!" are the requests they make in faltering tones. "Pray for me!" says one.

At night the scene is still more wondrous, for then men—old men, young men, earnest men—have taken possession of the auditorium. At these meetings Mr. Moody is at his best. Eleven thousand men packed in that old Hippodrome at one of the night gatherings in March and April. The gas lights shine in their eager faces. No political convention ever presented such a scene. Thousands arise and cry, "I will! I will!" when asked to enlist; "Amens!" sweep through the place like the rattling of musketry, and sometimes the ecstasy of religion becomes so manifest that long intervals of silent prayer are necessary in order to keep the sin-stricken within the bounds of needed self-restraint.

The numbers definitely brought to Christ in these meetings from 1876 to 1881 were never estimated by Mr. Moody. He was intolerant of that kind of statistics. When a minister asked him how many souls had been saved under his preaching, he only answered:

"I don't know anything about that, doctor. Thank God, I don't have to. I don't keep the Lamb's Book of Life."

Chapter 16

D. L. MOODY AS AN EVANGELIST: HIS CHARACTERISTICS AND METHODS,

By C. I. Scofield, D.D.

IT IS THE MARK of weak men that they break down under unusual responsibilities, of strong men that they are developed by them. The two Americans who in our generation had most in common, Lincoln and Grant, both came to the maturity of their powers under the pressure of immense labors and responsibilities. Both began with a modest estimate of their capacities; both came at last to a singularly humble self-confidence. So it may be said that under the testings of his great English campaign Mr. Moody came to the maturity of his powers. He grew in knowledge and in grace to the day of his death; but in mastery of assemblies, in readiness of resource, in capacity of leadership, in unfailing tact, and in strategic grasp and skill, he returned to America in the fullness of his great capacities.

Doubtless, also, his character had ripened and matured. Three supreme testings await strong men in this life: the testing of poverty and obscurity; of prosperity and applause; and of suffering. Many who enter life conscious, even though dimly, of great latent capacities, turn sour and bitter under neglect, narrow circumstances, and lack of appreciation. Others who pass that first trial successfully are corrupted or enfeebled by success and adulation. Many who stand erect alike in obscurity and success, fail utterly under the testing of suffering. Mr. Moody, by God's grace, passed unscathed through them all. Perhaps it has happened to few men, suddenly lifted into the fellowship of the noble and famous of the earth, to be so little moved from the serenity of their minds, the even tenor of their ways.

Doubtless this self-poise was in part an inheritance—the hill-town New Englander's habitual self-respect. But doubtless, too, Mr. Moody had so great a sense of the essential dignity of even the least of the sons of God, that he was little affected by earthly titles or personal fame.

At one of his great London meetings he was, as usual, superintending from the platform the seating of the immense audience. While so occupied, and at the moment when he was following with a rather anxious eye a couple of bewildered old ladies who were vainly seeking for front seats, a friend brought upon the platform a famous English earl.

"Glad to see you, Lord ——," said Mr. Moody. "Won't you please take a couple of chairs to those two old ladies down there?"

This the earl proceeded to do, to the consternation of his rather obsequious introducer.

On another occasion it was whispered to him, with some agitation, that a certain exalted personage had entered the hall.

Mr. Moody quietly replied:

"I hope she may be much blessed."

This independence, springing as it did from elevation and simplicity of character, and not at all from self-assertiveness, commended him to all classes in Great Britain. They found neither subserviency nor bumptiousness in this plain, strong Christian man.

All these qualities, previously but partially apprehended by his countrymen, became known through newspaper reports, and did much to prepare in America the remarkable outburst of confidence and esteem with which his return was greeted. In a very real sense, Christian America rose to receive him.

But the facts for once outran the rumor of them. It is not too much to say that as man, as preacher, as organizer, and as Christian strategist, the great 1876-1881 meetings revealed D. L. Moody as supreme.

In the superficial view it was always his generalship, his mastery of vast numbers of men gathered in meetings, which first impressed the observer; and for this reason his grip of his audience was not due in the first instance to his power as a preacher. Other men, as Whitefield and Wesley and the great Welsh field-preachers, have drawn vast audiences, and have in the end powerfully swayed them, however turbulent or tumultous they may have been when these great masters of the "royal art of preaching" rose to address them. But D. L. Moody never began to preach until he had gathered his audience into almost perfect *rapport* with himself. This was his unique distinction among other equally great preachers.

To accomplish this result he devised a method perfectly adapted to himself, but which in the hands of his imitators is by no means sure of success. Briefly, it was the conduct of a remarkably intense and spiritual preliminary service of song and prayer, interspersed with brief, pungent, characteristic sayings of his own. From the time he came before his great audiences to the moment when he rose to preach, he kept the entire body absorbingly occupied with something interesting. Singing by the great massed choir, by quartettes, duetists, soloists, and by the whole assembly, never ceased, except for prayer. But it would be an utter misapprehension to suppose that either his purpose or the actual result achieved was the entertainment of the people. His own manner showed at once his tremendous earnestness, his profound concern for souls.

The singing had a great and at times overpowering religious value. Before the evangelist rose, the throngs were already shaken, touched, persuaded. A great number of cases came to be known in which the momentous decision for Christ was actually made while Mr. Sankey was singing. Never was a more thoughtless criticism uttered than that Mr. Moody used music merely to attract.

But simple and obvious as seemed the plan of his introductory service, it was soon found, when the host of imitators began to use it, that like any other method in evangelistic work, it was worth little simply as a method. Apart from the purpose, and above all the power, it accomplished little.

When his almost unfailing spiritual discernment told him the time had come, he rose to preach.

D. L. Moody as a preacher was much criticized from the standpoint of academic homiletics. Nor would any think of defending his preaching method on that ground. But that for thirty-five continuous years, in the centers of culture and of active practical thought in the English-speaking world, this self-taught preacher drew the greatest audiences which have fronted any modern speaker on any theme—this fact, one would say, should suggest to teachers of homiletics that possibly they might learn something from him.

His method was devoid of mystery. Drawing his matter from the Scriptures, he utterly eschewed formal introduction, and plunged at once into the subject itself. That there were slips of grammar was most true; nor was there the slightest effort to suppress a nasal utterance. But he early came to the possession of a nervous Saxon vocabulary, and his strong sense taught him the value of the short sentence and of aphoristic forms.

Of all this the man himself, as he stood before his audience, was utterly unconscious. He was tremendously in earnest, absolutely sincere, perfectly incapable of phrase-making. It was his supreme possession by the Spirit, united with his powerful understanding, which were his safeguards against bathos, turgid rhetoric, pose, and artifice. Like all natural orators, he made great and effective use of illustration. And yet, it is doubtful if he ever used even the most telling illustration purely for effect.

He told an anecdote or referred to a Bible story or incident because it made his point clear.

Among his natural gifts were humor, always refined, pathos, and a descriptive power which was due to his imagination. Few men ever equaled him in ability to summon before an audience the whole setting of a Bible incident. And he had the sovereign grace of brevity. He knew when to stop, and he never weakened his sermon at the close by recapitulation.

That all these rare excellencies of public discourse might have been within the mastery of this man, and that he still might have failed utterly of his purpose apart from the mighty power of the baptizing Spirit, is wholly true; but it is right to say that in this humble servant of Jesus, the Spirit had the using of one of the great natural preachers of all time.

Chapter 17

DAILY LIFE AT NORTHFIELD, AS CITIZEN AND NEIGHBOR

THE CAREER of a public man awakens interest in his manner of life behind the scenes. People want to know how the man whom they see lives at home, and what his neighbors think of him.

No man's private life will stand scrutiny better than D. L. Moody's, whether you consider him in the role of parent, neighbor, or friend. Always and throughout everything, he was a true Christian, a true man.

His Chicago home had been burned in the fire of 1871. The winter following he slept in the North Side Tabernacle, while his wife and family stayed with friends. The missions in England occupied four years more, and when he returned to America he was still without a home.

Under these circumstances he went to Northfield to see his mother, and decided to make his permanent home there, in order to be near her when not engaged in evangelistic labors. He purchased an old homestead within a stone's-throw of his birthplace.

Northfield is a typical New England town, with a history running back more than two hundred years, beautifully situated on the banks of the Connecticut at the junction of the three States of Massachusetts, New Hampshire, and Vermont. From Mr. Moody's front porch a scene of great quiet beauty extends, embracing the rich valley of the Connecticut, with the Green Mountains beyond.

As the years went by, Mr. Moody transformed the village into a veritable Mecca by establishing schools, conferences, and other enterprises, of which only brief mention can be made.

Northfield Seminary for young women was formally opened on November 3, 1879.

Mount Hermon School for young men was projected in 1879, and opened for instruction on May 4, 1881.

The first General Conference for Christian Workers was held in 1880.

The first World's Student Conference was held in 1886.

The Northfield Training School for women was opened in 1890.

The first Women's Conference was organized in 1893.

The magazine, *Northfield Echoes,* was established in 1894.

The General Eastern Depot of the Bible Institute Colportage Association, of Chicago, was opened in 1895.

Camp Northfield, for men, was organized in 1896.

Of later years it was Mr. Moody's custom to spend the months from October to April (inclusive) in evangelistic work. With what pleasure his return to

Northfield about May 1 was looked forward to by his students and family! There was no place he loved more than Northfield, and he always regretted to have to leave for even short absences during the summer months. Writing from New York City in December, 1896, he said:

"The city is no place for me. If it was not for the work I am called to do I would never show my head in this city, or any other, again. It is a rush all the time, and a drive. Oh, the quiet days at Northfield, how I long for them!"

He was an early riser. He generally rose about daybreak in summer, devoting the early hours to Bible study and communion with God. He used to say that one who followed this plan could not get more than twenty-four hours away from God.

It often happened, however, that some matter of business would demand attention before breakfast, and perhaps he would be found bursting into the kitchen at Mount Hermon School (four miles distant from his home) by seven o'clock, inspecting the food that was being prepared for breakfast, and tasting one dish and another to assure himself of their quality. Or perhaps he would drive up to his own garden to get some eggs or vegetables for breakfast.

Breakfast with the family at 7:30, and immediately afterward family prayers, which house servants and hired men also attended. Mr. Moody read a passage of Scripture and then prayed simply and earnestly.

While the schools were still in session, he usually conducted chapel exercises at the Seminary at 9 A.M.

and at Mount Hermon School at noon. At these brief services, lasting about twenty minutes, he came into close heart relations with his students in spiritual things. He usually dealt with fundamental doctrines—intensely practical and personal talks, and quite informal. It was his supreme object to help his students into the deeper things of God, and he was always ready to meet those who were anxious about their spiritual condition.

The last mornings he spent with the students were occupied with the theme "Eternal Life."

Returning from the chapel at Mount Hermon School, dinner was served at one o'clock. By this time the morning mail had been delivered.

His correspondence was quite large, and he made it a point to open every letter himself. Letters connected with the different schools were separated and given to subordinates, and general letters were usually handed to his secretary. In special cases he would indicate by brief notes what reply should be made. Letters received prompt attention—even those from religious and other cranks were usually courteously acknowledged.

The remaining hours of the day were filled in with an enormous amount of work and play. He gave personal attention to the innumerable details of the large institutions at Northfield, Mount Hermon, and Chicago; for it must be remembered that in addition to local interests he kept his hand on the Chicago Bible Institute, with its organizations for aggressive Christian work in prisons, in the army camps, as well as in the ordinary avenues in which his Colportage Association worked.

He gave careful attention to the planning of the summer conventions. It has often been remarked that one charm of these great gatherings was their freshness and spontaneity. This is true of the result, but the result is achieved by months of painstaking preparations and arrangement of details.

"In nothing, perhaps, is Mr. Moody's genius for command more manifest than in his capacity for detail," wrote a friend. "Nothing is too minute for his best thought, for he knows how much results depend on little things. Along with this genius for details goes remarkable quickness of insight and decision."

Mr. Moody used to perform the work of about ten men. How he ever did it was a mystery until one realized (1) his absolute dependence upon God for guidance as to details, and his consequent freedom from anxiety as to the outcome; (2) his genius to command; (3) his faculty of doing promptly what had to be attended to personally, and of passing over to his subordinates and associates such details as they were competent to carry out.

How often he would say in some difficult case: "Oh, I wish I could see Christ face to face for five minutes and ask Him what He would do!"

All these matters were dealt with during his summer "rest"; but his real relaxation has not yet been mentioned. He thought that every man should have some hobby to divert his mind. Mr. Moody's hobby was his garden and his chickens. He must have *life;* he loved to see things grow. "Send me a good farm letter," he would frequently write home.

A letter exists that would lead one to think that he was starting a farm instead of a boys' school at Mount Hermon:

"I bought twenty-five old sheep and twenty-five lambs for the boys' school," he wrote, "and turned the cows over there from my barn and Smith's, so we have eight cows over there now, and will have seventy-five hens there soon. One of the turkeys is setting. I am going to have some geese over there to make things lively. We have, or will have to-morrow night, seven boys. Am expecting more next week."

His garden was hardly conducted on a profitable basis. Here he experimented with asparagus and other vegetables, for the benefit of the schools. He tried to be first in the neighborhood with the different crops. He was greatly pleased to have peas from his garden in September. He kept a dozen or more families supplied daily with fresh vegetables during the summer months.

Feeding his chickens furnished him with an excuse for exercise, as he had to walk about half a mile and back twice daily to feed them. Each spring he hatched chickens by the hundred—sometimes by the thousand—in incubators.

The following is an estimate of D. L. Moody as a citizen and neighbor, taken by permission from the county paper:

> The old proverb, "A prophet is not without honor save in his own country," cannot be said of D. L. Moody, for surely no person could be more sincerely loved and honored by his townsmen than was he. Expressions of sorrow are

heard from all classes of people in the town, and could each tribute be represented by a blossom on his grave, it would be piled high with flowers. His townsmen have been proud of him as a citizen, as a man, and as a religious worker. Although not all of them have indorsed his religious belief, they have thoroughly believed in his honesty of purpose and sincerity, and are convinced that the results of his lifework will be lasting and of inestimable value to future generations. They know that Northfield has been changed from a quiet farming town, with corresponding disadvantages, to a thrifty village with a steady growth; and that there and at Mount Hermon have been established two of the best fitting-schools in the State, all through the energy and perseverance of this man. Every effort has been made by him to bring these schools within the reach of the boys and girls of the town, and many an ambitious father and mother have been able to educate their children through his efforts.

Last summer he was told of a woman who was supporting her family by taking in washing, that her daughter was ready for the Seminary, but she almost despaired of her ability to send her there. Mr. Moody instantly replied: "Tell the principal to put her on the free list, and find her a room in the buildings. The town girls must be helped first."

This is only one instance of many similar ones. Under certain provisions, he offered every Northfield and Gill boy free tuition for the first year at Mount Hermon, and several boys availed themselves of this opportunity each year since.

He was instantly alert and ready with money and work to forward any plans to benefit the town. At the time the Village Improvement Society was formed, he subscribed one hundred dollars to improve the street, knowing that it would be expended in a part of the village remote from the school and his residence. Every year since its formation he has given generously of money, and has also offered valuable advice and wise suggestions.

He was very proud of the magnificent trees of the village, and nothing irritated him more than any attempt to injure them. He caused to be set a large number of trees and shrubs about his place and on the Seminary grounds. It must have been very gratifying for him to see Seminary Hill in all its June splendor, knowing that in his childhood it was considered one of the most barren places in town. One old man once said that that sidehill wouldn't bear white beans, when he was a boy.

He was a kind neighbor, sickness and trouble finding him ready with sympathy and material help. The delicacies of his garden and fruit orchard found their way into many a humble home. He encouraged his wife and daughter to interest themselves in helping the sick and needy in all parts of the town.

During the autumn, when fruit was abundant, the Seminary girls were given free access to his orchard and grapery, to eat and carry baskets full to their rooms. Each fall he gave all the surplus apples on his own and the Seminary campus, and solicited from neighboring farmers to the extent of hundreds of bushels, which were distributed among the poor in Boston and New York.

He had a strong aversion to committees. An organization was being effected in the town hall, and a motion was made to appoint certain committees. Mr. Moody rose and said: "We don't want committees. When you want anything done, tell Mr. So-and-so to do it, and you will accomplish something. One is enough to constitute any committee. If there had been a committee appointed, Noah's ark would never have been built."

He used to spend hours "puttering around" his hen-houses and garden (as he used to express it), but all the time his mind was ready to deal with more important things, and some fellow worker or subordinate was frequently at his side, discussing plans.

He spent the evenings with his family when no meetings demanded his presence. He kept in touch with the progress of the world by reading the daily papers. He was no ascetic. No work was so important as to make him neglect his family duties and privileges. He took keen interest in the doings of his sons at school and college, and shared their joys and excitements. In his younger manhood he was a very swift runner, and could hold his own with his Chicago Sunday-school scholars.

Rev. F. B. Meyer once called him the most fearless of whips. "Where have I not been in that buggy? It is the most natural thing in the world for the driver to leave the road, climb over a ditch and hedge, and make straight for the top of a grassy slope because he wanted to show you a view, or descend a plowed field into a glen to explain his method of raising water from the spring to Mount Hermon School."

Chapter 18

VISIT TO THE HOLY LAND

A MAN OF SUCH energetic spirit as Mr. Moody found very little opportunity for holidays. He sacredly tried to observe one day in the seven as a Sabbath, but otherwise he was almost constantly occupied, except when journeying—and even then people recognized him and sought his spiritual advice, and were not denied. Of late years, with the multiplication of his schools, conferences, and other organizations for promoting the cause of Christ, there was less and less opportunity for withdrawing for any length of time from active participation in their control.

In the spring of 1892, Mr. Moody was able to take a well-deserved holiday and at the same time gratify an old longing to visit the Holy Land. The summer preceding, Dr. John Smith, of Edinburgh, had come to America with a huge roll of invitations from ministers of Scotland, asking Mr. Moody to visit that country again. He left America in October, 1891, and with Mr. Sankey, held short meetings in ninety-nine towns in Scotland during the winter. This was his last visit to Scotland.

In April, 1892, he was invited by Mr. and Mrs. Peter McKinnon, of Scotland, to go to Palestine.

From Paris he wrote to his mother, "I have a great desire to see the city of gold." Accompanied by his wife and his younger son Paul, he joined the Mc-Kinnons in Rome.

Mr. Moody's enjoyment of Rome was intense. Every place which could be verified as being in any way connected with the apostle Paul (his greatest Bible hero, next to our Lord) was carefully sought out. The Appian Way was visited, and when the original pavement was reached he insisted on alighting from the carriage and going on foot over the stones which Paul had trodden. The ruins of Nero's palace on the Palatine Hill had far more attraction for him than Peter's, or any of the spectacles of modern Rome.

The party sailed in one of Mr. McKinnon's liners, and landed at Port Said. It was necessary to sail down the Suez Canal as far as Ismalia, and thence take train to Alexandria. Writing from Port Said, Mr. Moody said:

"We are now near where the children of Israel passed when they went out of Egypt. The country is sandy and barren, but the canal is a wonder, and it seems strange to be in this land of the Pharaohs, of Moses and Aaron and Joseph."

The day after his arrival in Jerusalem, which happened to be Easter Sunday, he spoke from the summit of the new (or Gordon) Calvary on the text: "As the mountains are round about Jerusalem, so the Lord is round about his people from henceforth even forever"—pointing to Hermon, Olivet, and the mountains of Moab, all in sight from where he stood. It was afterward found that he had unwittingly spoken in the midst of a Mohammedan cemetery, and a little feeling was unfortunately aroused. It was not thought wise to repeat the mistake, so the following Sunday he preached in a recess in the side of the hill. Several hundreds of all races and creeds attended these meetings.

The weekdays were spent in visiting places of interest in Jerusalem and the immediate vicinity. One day was devoted to Hebron. In Jerusalem all the sacred spots, like the Holy Sepulcher, were too uncertain or else too transformed by tawdriness to please. His favorite places were the Mount of Olives, to which he repeatedly returned, and the little village of Bethany, over the brow of the hill. Here, at any rate, he knew he was in the midst of scenes where his Master had often walked.

At Bethany he told his dragoman to ask if there were any Marys and Marthas among the children. The Arabic equivalents of these names were instantly claimed by a number, and nobody enjoyed the joke more than himself when it was explained that most of the "Miriams" and "Marthas" were boys.

Being unable to ride horseback, Mr. Moody's travels in Palestine were limited; but he was an energetic sightseer.

The native children in Jerusalem amused him greatly. On his exit from the hotel he would invariably be surrounded by a crowd of ragged little Arabs, and he entertained himself by giving them backsheesh. The older natives also interested him, and he conversed with them constantly, question-

ing them as to their manner of living. By the end
of the week he was well informed concerning the
manner of life of the people, the condition of agri-
culture, the system of government, and a dozen and
one other things.

Leaving Palestine, Mr. Moody and those with
him went to Egypt. Several days were spent in
Cairo, visiting the pyramids and other points of interest, and in the first week of May the party left
for Italy. May was spent in Naples and Florence,
the Italian lakes and Switzerland, and by the end
of the month he was again in England, having been
absent for two months, probably the longest vaca-
tion he had taken since he entered business as a boy
of seventeen. It was not an unbroken rest, however,
for he had preached at Rome, Jerusalem, Cairo,
Naples, and Paris, sometimes twice a day, besides
having conducted numerous Bible readings, in
compliance with the importunities of English and
American friends, who recognized him wherever
he went. Moreover, he used to lead the most unlikely people on the most unlikely occasions into
direct personal talk regarding their spiritual condition.

"Mr. Moody," said a titled lady to him, "no one
ever talked to me like this before."

"Then it is quite time somebody did so," he replied; and they remained good friends.

His visit to the Holy Land remained a living
memory with him. He constantly referred to it in
private conversation and public discourse, regret-
ting, on the one hand, the condition of Palestine,

which he believed was in accord with prophecy, and on the other hand looking forward with joy to its restoration, when the feet of the Messiah shall stand once more on Mount Olivet.

Chapter 19

FACING DEATH ON THE ATLANTIC

ON HIS RETURN to England he again "got in harness," and preached in and around London. In August he crossed to Ireland, and preached in a number of centers there. Returning to America with his elder son in November, he had his memorable experience on board the North German Lloyd liner, the "Spree," an experience as thrilling as any in the record of Atlantic ocean accidents.

He took passage from Southampton, England, early in November. He reported:

> My last day in London was a pleasant one; a day of promise it might have been called, for the sun shone brightly after some of those dark, foggy days so common. A company of friends gathered at the station to see me off, and I suggested that they should sing my favorite song, "Then shall my heart keep singing," but they said that they did not feel like singing that just then. I was the only one in the group who seemed to feel like singing.
>
> When about three days on our voyage, I remember, I was lying on my couch, as I generally do at sea, congratulating myself on my good for-

126

tune, and feeling very thankful to God. I considered myself a very fortunate man, for in all my extensive travels by land and sea I had never been in any accident of a serious nature.

Suddenly I was startled by a terrible crash and shock, as if the vessel had been driven on a rock. I did not at first feel much anxiety—perhaps I was too ill to think about it. My son jumped from his berth, and rushed on deck. He was back again in a few moments saying that the shaft was broken and the vessel was sinking. I did not at first believe it could be so bad, but concluded to dress and go on deck. The report was only too true. The captain told the affrighted passengers, who had rushed on deck, that there was no danger, and some of the second-cabin passengers returned to their berths, only to be driven out again by the in-rushing water, leaving everything behind them.

The officers and crew did all they could to save the vessel. But it was soon found that the pumps were useless, for the water poured into the ship too rapidly to be controlled. There was nothing more in the power of man to do. We were utterly helpless. We could only stand still on the poor, drifting sinking ship and look into our watery graves.

All this time, unknown to the passengers, the officers were making preparations for the last resort. The lifeboats were all put in readiness, provisions prepared, life preservers in hand, the officers armed with revolvers to enforce their orders, and the question was evidently being debated in their mind whether to launch the boats at once, or wait. The sea was so heavy that the boats could hardly survive. Two of the passengers had

loaded revolvers ready to blow out their brains
if the vessel should go down, preferring death by
bullet to death by drowning.

At noon the captain told us that he had the
water under control, and was in hopes of drifting
in the way of some passing vessel. The ship's bow
was now high in the air, the stern seemed to settle more and more. The sea was very rough, and
the ship rolled from side to side with fearful
lurches. If she had pitched violently but once,
the bulkheads must have burst, and the end
come. The captain tried to keep up hope by
telling us we should probably drift in the way of
a ship by three o'clock that Saturday afternoon,
but the night closed upon us without a sign of
a sail.

That was an awful night, the darkest in all our
lives! Seven hundred men, women, and children
waiting for the doom that was settling upon us!
No one dared to sleep. We were all together in
the saloon of the first cabin—Jews, Protestants,
Catholics, and skeptics—although I doubt if at
that time there were any skeptics among us. The
agony and suspense were too great for words.
With blanched faces and trembling hearts the
passengers looked at one another, as if trying to
read what no one dared to speak. Rockets flamed
into the sky, but there was no answer. We were
drifting out of the track of the great steamers.
Every hour seemed to increase our danger.

Sunday morning dawned without help or
hope. Up to that time no suggestion of religious
services had been made. To have done that would
almost certainly have produced a panic. In the
awful suspense and dread that prevailed, a word
about religion would have suggested the most

terrible things to the passengers. But as that second night came on I asked General O. O. Howard, who was with us, to secure the captain's permission for a service in the saloon. The captain said: "Most certainly; I am that kind, too."

We gave notice of the meeting, and to our surprise nearly every passenger attended, and I think everybody prayed, skeptics and all.

With one arm clasping a pillar to steady myself on the reeling vessel, I tried to read the Ninety-first Psalm, and we prayed that God would still the raging of the sea and bring us to our desired haven. It was a new psalm to me from that hour. The eleventh verse touched me very deeply. It was like a voice of divine assurance, and it seemed a very real thing as I read: "He shall give his angels charge over thee, to keep thee in all thy ways." Surely He did it. I read also from Psalm 107:20-31. One lady thought those words must have been written for the occasion, and afterward asked to see the Bible for herself. A German translated verse by verse as I read, for the benefit of his countrymen.

I was passing through a new experience. I had thought myself superior to the fear of death. I had often preached on the subject, and urged Christians to realize this victory of faith. During the Civil War I had been under fire without fear. I was in Chicago during the great cholera epidemic, and went around with the doctors visiting the sick and dying. Where they could go to look after the *bodies* of men I said I could go to look after their *souls*. I remember a case of smallpox where the flesh had literally dropped away from the backbone, yet I went to the bedside of that poor sufferer again and again, with

Bible and prayer for Jesus' sake. In all this I
had no fear of death.

But on the sinking ship it was different. There
was no cloud between my soul and my Saviour.
I knew my sins had been put away, and that if I
died there it would be only to wake up in Heav-
en. That was all settled long ago. But as my
thoughts went out to my loved ones at home—
my wife and children, my friends on both sides
of the sea, the schools and all the interests so
dear to me—and as I realized that perhaps the
next hour would separate me forever from all
these, so far as this world was concerned, I confess it almost broke me down. It was the darkest
hour of my life!

I could not endure it. I must have relief, and
relief came in prayer. God heard my cry, and enabled me to say, from the depth of my soul: "Thy
will be done!" Sweet peace came to my heart.
Let it be "Northfield or Heaven," it made no dif-
ference now. I went to bed and almost immediately fell asleep, and never slept more soundly in
all my life. Out of the depths I cried unto the
Lord, and He heard me and delivered me from
all my fears. I can no more doubt that God gave
answer to my prayer for relief than I can doubt
my own existence.

About three o'clock at night I was aroused
from my sound sleep by the voice of my son.
"Come on deck, Father," he said. I followed
him, and he pointed to a light, rising and sinking on the sea. It was a messenger of deliverance
to us. It proved to be the light of the steamer
"Lake Huron," whose lookout had seen our flam-
ing signals of distress, and supposed it was a
vessel in flames. Oh, the joy of that moment,

when those seven hundred despairing passengers beheld the approaching ship! Who can ever forget it?

But now the question was, Can this small steamer tow the helpless "Spree" a thousand miles to Queenstown? Every moment was watched with the intensest anxiety and prayer. It was a brave and perilous undertaking. The two vessels were at last connected by two great cables. If a storm arose these would snap like thread, and we must be left to our fate. But I had no fear. God would finish the work He had begun. The waves were calmed; the cables held; the steamer moved in the wake of the "Huron." There were storms all about us, but they came not nigh our broken ship. Seven days after the accident, by the good hand of our God upon us, we were able to hold a joyous thanksgiving service in the harbor of Queenstown. The rescuing ship that God sent to us in our distress had just sufficient power to tow our ship, and just enough coal to take her into port! Less would have been insufficient. Her captain, a man of prayer, besought God's help to enable them to accomplish their dangerous and difficult task. God answered the united prayer of the distressed voyagers, and brought them to their desired haven.

The nervous strain of those eight days and nights of suspense was something fearful. It was more than anyone could long endure without help. The minds of several passengers gave way under the strain. A young Austrian, who had left his betrothed in Vienna, leaped overboard in despair, and was drowned before our eyes in spite of all we could do. It was a most pathetic sight to see a young mother, with two beautiful chil-

dren, sitting in dumb anguish during the first
forty-eight hours, never taking her eyes off her
little ones; and if the ship had gone down, I have
no doubt she would have gathered them to her
bosom and gone down with them in her arms.
There was a Russian Jew, who had taken passage without the knowledge of his relatives at
home. It was pitiful to see his distress, as he confessed his sin, beat his breast, and denounced
himself as the Jonah of the company. Kneeling
upon the deck, with tears streaming down his
cheeks, he cried to Jehovah not to visit the punishment of his sin upon all those unfortunate
people.

Mr. Moody always spoke with profound respect
and gratitude of the courage and gallantry of the
officers and crew of the "Spree."

General O. O. Howard, who had faced danger
and death many times during the Civil War, and
who knew what courage meant, testified to the
nerve and courage exhibited by Mr. Moody during
those awful hours.

Spending Saturday night in Queenstown, Mr.
Moody sailed for America on the "Etruria" next
day, and reached New York safely the following
Saturday.

What a reception he got when he reached home
at ten o'clock that night! As the train passed
through Mount Hermon Station, three hundred
students and teachers from that school swarmed in
and around the train, with torches, music, and
cheers to welcome their friend. At the next station
he was met on alighting by another company of

friends. The buildings of Northfield Seminary, as well as many private dwellings, were ablaze with innumerable lights in the windows. It seemed as if everyone who loved him meant to let him know it, and to give him an ovation on his rescue from the very jaws of death.

Chapter 20

WITHIN THE FAMILY CIRCLE

"Has Grandpa gone to Jesus' house?"

"Yes."

"Where Dwight and Irene are?"

"Yes."

"Well, I want to go there too, and I'll just hug Grandpa when I see him, and we'll play together."

The questionings of a four-year-old little girl when she was told she would never see her grandfather any more down here, reveal a side of Mr. Moody's nature that was little known to the general public.

A new era began in his life with the marriage of his only daughter and elder son, both in 1894. Joys and sorrows, health and sickness, came hand in hand. In those last six years there were four births in his immediate family—four grandchildren; and four deaths—his mother, his wife's mother, and two of the grandchildren.

D. L. Moody was a loving, dutiful son. Hardly a week passed, from the time he left home in 1854, without his writing to his mother, or sending her newspaper clippings about his work. He settled in Northfield in 1875 so as to be near her. Every day, when he was in town, it was his delight to call upon her, generally bringing her some little delicacy, or some vegetables from his garden. He added to the old homestead a sunny room where she sat in her later years, a mother in Israel, glad because of the good works God was performing through her son.

Next to his wife, he consulted his mother more than any other living being.

One of the greatest joys of his life was to see his mother publicly confess Christ, and join the evangelical church. He was to preach that Sunday morning in 1876 in the old Congregational Church at Northfield. His subject was the Fifty-first Psalm. "Religion is a personal matter," he said. "David prayed that God would wash *him,* not his clothes; and have mercy upon *him.*" He sketched graphically the journey of life; some in the audience were nearing the top of the hill; others were already going down the other side. When he had finished preaching, he made a tender appeal to all to accept his Saviour as their Saviour. His mother sat near the front, and was one of the first to rise for prayer. When he saw her, tears of joy filled his eyes, his voice choked, and turning to B. F. Jacobs, of Chicago, who was sitting beside him on the platform, he asked him to pray, saying:

"That's my mother!"

Her birthday fell on the same day as his own (February 5) , and his letters on successive anniversaries were peculiarly tender.

"You and I have now passed one more milestone on our way from earth to Heaven. We have both reason to thank God for all His goodness to us."

"By the time you get this letter," he wrote from

Perth, Scotland, in 1892, "you will be passing another milestone that will bring you nearer the Eternal City. I want to send you my best wishes for the
new year you will be starting out on. I hope it will
be full of joy and sunshine and peace."

The last birthday letter he wrote her was from
San Antonio, Texas, on February 2, 1895:

"By the time this letter gets to you, you will have
entered into your ninety-first year. Only think,
when you entered this world, Napoleon was fighting his great battles! It seems a long time, as you
look at the history that has been made. Nations
have risen and fallen. Some have come and gone.
Yet you live, and have all your faculties and good
health. You have much to praise God for, and all
your children rejoice to think you have been spared
to us so long."

"Fifty years I have been coming back to Northfield," said he, "and have always been glad to get
back. When I get within fifty miles of home I grow
restless, and walk up and down the car. It seems as
if the train will never get to Northfield. When I
came back after dark, I always looked to see the
light in mother's window."

On January 26, 1896, she fell on sleep. "Friends,"
said Mr. Moody at her funeral, "it is not a time of
mourning. We are proud that we had such a
mother. We have a wonderful legacy left us. . . .
God bless you, Mother; we love you still. Death has
only increased our love. Good-by for a little while."

The joy of being a grandparent had become his a
few months previously, when Irene Moody was

born on August 20, 1895, and Emma Fitt on December 16 following.

"Do you know I have a granddaughter? I am taking a present over to her," he shouted from his buggy to a summer visitor that August morning, pointing to a basket of doughnuts. He was happy as a schoolboy on a holiday, and told the news to everybody he met. Later that day he made a second trip to Mount Hermon to see the baby, this time bringing over an immense cauliflower, the best his garden had produced.

A letter he wrote to Emma a year later reveals his heart:

December 10, 1896.

In six days you will be one year old, and your grandmother will make you a cake, and have it all frosted over with white sugar, and they will put one tiny little candle on it. . . . It will be one year ago next Tuesday night I was sitting up for your grandmother, and when it got past midnight I thought I would go and see why she did not come home, and I heard you cry for the first time. The tears of joy came to my eyes, and I have thought a great deal of you ever since. Soon after, my mother died, and you seemed to come to take her place, and you have been a dear, good little girl. . . .

I am going to steal up to your home next summer and take you out riding before your parents get up. Only think, of some fine June morning, we can go up Lovers' Retreat. The birds will sing you a beautiful song. What times we will have together! I get real homesick thinking about it . . .

And now, my dear Emma, I am praying for you that the Lord will watch over you day and night, and keep you from all harm. You will never know how much your grandfather loves you. I shall be glad to get you into my arms again.

His playful nature is exhibited in the first letter he wrote little Emma, on January 7, 1896, when she was three weeks old:

This is my first letter to my dear little grand-child. I wanted to get a letter to you before you got your first tooth. Hurry up and get them before the hot weather comes on, for I will get you some candy, and you will want teeth to eat it. I want you to hurry up and grow, so I can come early mornings and take you out riding when your father and mother are fast asleep. We will slip off over the river to see Irene, and have some good times. Your mother is so proud of you, and your nurse is so fussy. Only think, Emma, what your mother said the other day—I, your grandfather, could not kiss you on your lips! Did you ever hear anything like that! But I got a kiss on your lips all the same, and I will get a good many more when I get home.

A few months later he wrote:

I have just heard that the milk you get at my house does not agree with you. Now I think the fault is not with the milk, but with the cooks. You know, or you should be old enough to know, that when you cook milk and put it in a bottle and put a black rubber nipple on it—you will be disgusted when you get a little older and know how your parents have treated you! You must not blame my old cow, for she is as good as she can be. I do not want to turn you against your parents, but if they do not treat you right, slip down to my house and get some doughnuts and icecream.

And so his loving heart went out to his grand-children, and they in return loved none better than him. In the summer months he would usually be seen with one or more of them seated beside him as he drove around town.

"He has learned to perfection the art of being a grandfather," wrote a friend. "I saw him one morning driving with his little four-year-old grand-daughter into the yard of his house. The child had gone to sleep in the buggy, leaning against him. Rather than disturb her, he had the horse gently unharnessed and taken away, while they sat on. Presently he, too, was overcome with sleep."

But God had ordained something other than un-broken joy. His only grandson and namesake, who was born on November 7, 1897, was taken home on November 30, 1898, while he was absent in Colo-rado. Irene, his first grandchild followed her baby brother on August 22, 1899 (aged four years and two days), after a protracted and unusually per-sistent attack of pneumonia, which soon developed into consumption.

COLORADO SPRINGS, COLO.

. . . I know Dwight is having a good time, and we should rejoice with him. What would the mansions be without children? And he has gone to help get things ready for his parents. You know the Master said: "The last shall be first."

He was the last to come into our circle, and he is the first to go up there! So safe, so free from all the sorrow that we are passing through! I do thank God for such a life. It was nearly all smiles and sunshine. What a glorified body he will have, and with what joy he will await your coming! God does not give us such strong love for each other for a few days or years, but it is going to last forever, and you will have the dear little man with you for ages and ages, and love will keep increasing. The master had need of him, or He would never have called him; and you should feel highly honored that you had anything in your home that He wanted.

I cannot think of him as belonging to earth. The more I think of him the more I think he was only sent to us to draw us all closer to each other and up to the world of light and joy. I could not wish him back, if he could have all earth could give him. And then the thought that the Saviour will take such good care of him! No going astray; no sickness; no death. Dear, dear little fellow! I love to think of him, so sweet, so safe, and so lovely! His life was not only blameless, but faultless; and if his life here was so sweet, what will it be up there? I believe the only thing he took away from earth was that sweet smile, and I have no doubt that when he saw the Saviour he smiled as he did when he saw you. My heart goes up to God often for you, and the word that keeps coming to my mind is this: "It is well with the child." Only think of his translation! Thank God, Dwight is safe at home, and we will all of us see him soon. Your loving father,

D. L. MOODY.

Just before the close of Irene's funeral service, Mr. Moody rose and spoke:

> I would like to say a few words, if I can trust myself. I have been thinking this morning about the aged prophet waiting in the valley of the Jordan, so many years ago, for the chariot of God to take him home. The chariot of God came down to the Connecticut valley yesterday morning about half-past six, and took our little Irene home. The one was taken at the end of years of active service; the other at the early dawn of youth. But the service of the prophet was no more complete than that of the little handmaid of the Lord, for God called both, and He never interrupts the service of His own.
>
> Irene has finished her course. Her work was well wrought on earth. She has accomplished more than many in their threescore years and ten. We would not have her back, although her voice was the sweetest voice I ever heard on earth. She never met me once since she was three months old, until the last few days of pain, without a smile. But Christ had some service for her above. My life has been made much better by her ministry here on earth. She has made us all better.
>
> The last few days have been blessed days to me. I have learned many new and precious lessons. She was very fond of riding with me, and on Monday morning she asked me to take her driving, and at 6:30 we were out together. She never looked more beautiful. She was just ripening for Heaven. She was too fair for this earth.
>
> I thank God this morning for the hope of immortality. I know I shall see her in the morning,

more beautiful in her resurrection glory than she was here.

God filled up his cup once more when a fourth grandchild was born on November 13, 1899, four days before he broke down at Kansas City. "Thankful for the good news," he telegraphed his son; "may she become famous in the kingdom of Heaven is the prayer of her grandfather"; and then he wrote:

"I am full of praise and thanksgiving today. . . . Dear little child, I already feel my heart going out to her! Kiss the mother and the dear baby for me. . . . Thank God for another grandchild!"

The same day he wrote his other surviving grandchild, Emma Fitt, one of those simple, loving letters that were so characteristic of him:

My dear Emma: I am glad that you have a little cousin. Will you kiss her for me, and will you show her your grandfather's picture [referring to a newspaper clipping he enclosed]? I do not think she will know me, but you can tell her all about me, so she will know me when she gets older, and we will play together with her. I am going to send her a little kiss, just one little one.

Your grandfather,

D. L. Moody

I will put the kiss in a little box, 💌, and you can take it to her.

Little Mary, the newborn babe, was carried to her grandfather's home ten days later. She never knew him, but the family kept precious letters for her.

Chapter 21

LAST EVANGELISTIC MISSION

MR. MOODY LEFT HOME for the last time on November 8, 1899. His family had no suspicion that he was not in usual health and strength.

He had engaged to conduct a week's meetings in Kansas City, Missouri. On his way thither he stopped over in Philadelphia, to see about a building they were erecting for him there for a series of meetings similar to his great meetings in 1875-76. He also stopped over at Chicago for a few hours, to attend to some business at the Bible Institute. Two addresses he delivered to the students were marked by unusual power.

He reached Kansas City a sick man. When some friends called on him at the hotel, he excused himself from rising, saying that he was tired. The first afternoon three of his old Mount Hermon students, C. M. Vining, Rev. D. Baines-Griffiths, and C. S. Bishop, took him a drive around the city. He seemed in good spirits, but they saw that he was not quite himself.

The great auditorium in which the meetings were held was estimated to hold easily fifteen thousand people. They say that fully that number attended his first Sunday meetings, while thousands were unable to gain admittance.

It was a thrilling spectacle. The great arena, like a valley filled with upturned faces, and the balconies thronged like receding hillsides covered with a countless multitude—and a solemn silence hovering over them all! Alone in that great assemblage stood Mr. Moody, at the front end of the extended platform. His voice sounded as though he was talking confidentially to a man in the eighth or tenth row, and without effort it carried to every part of the building.

He said later that the building did not tax his efforts in preaching.

Before commencing his sermon that first afternoon a characteristic incident happened. He raised in his hand a printed slip of hymns that had been distributed by the ushers, and said:

"Let everyone who has one of these slips hold it up."

Thousands of slips were raised aloft.

"Now sit on them," said he; and people laughed as they put the papers where their rustling should not disturb the meeting.

He preached both afternoon and evening on "Sowing and Reaping," from the text:

Be not deceived; God is not mocked; for whatsoever a man soweth, that shall he also reap; for he that soweth to his flesh, shall of the flesh reap corruption; but he that soweth to the Spirit, shall of the Spirit reap life everlasting. (Gal. 6: 7, 8.)

In conversation with Mr. Vining he talked of the institutions he had founded, and said the work in

Kansas City was, he believed, one of the greatest God had given him to do. He spoke of the bereavements that had occurred in his family during the past year, and picking up a copy of his book, *Thoughts from My Library,* he read a selection. It comments on the text Psalm 30:5: "Weeping may endure for a night, but joy cometh in the morning." The extract ends with the words:

"I have heard it in the Land of Light from which I come. There is a time approaching, steadily if not quickly, when the Lord will wipe away tears from all faces. This weary world shall obtain joy and gladness at last, and sorrow and sighing shall flee away. 'Wherefore comfort one another with these words.'"

Thursday, November 16, was the day on which he preached for the last time.

On the afternoon of that day his subject was "Grace in a Threefold Aspect":

> For the grace of God that bringeth salvation hath appeared to all men, teaching us that, denying ungodliness and worldly lusts, we should live soberly, righteously, and godly in this present world; looking for that blessed hope, and the glorious appearing of the Great God and our Saviour Jesus Christ, who gave himself for us, that he might redeem us from all iniquity, and purify unto himself a peculiar people, zealous of good works (Titus 2:11-14).

That last night Convention Hall was well filled. Mr. Moody showed no signs of exhaustion.

His last sermon on earth was on "Excuses." He

read the parable as found in Luke 14:16-24, beginning:

> Then said he unto him: A certain man made a great supper, and bade many; and sent his servant at supper time to say to them that were bidden, Come; for all things are now ready. And they all with one consent began to make excuse.

Had he known that this was to be his last sermon could he have made a more urgent and characteristic appeal in closing:

> Suppose we should write out tonight this excuse, how would it sound? *"To the King of Heaven: While sitting in Convention Hall, Kansas City, Mo., November 16, 1899, I received a very pressing invitation from one of your servants to be present at the marriage supper of your only begotten Son. I PRAY THEE HAVE ME EXCUSED."*
> Would you sign that, young man? Would you, mother? Would you come up to the reporter's table, take a pen and put your name down to such an excuse? You would say, "Let my right hand forget its cunning, and my tongue cleave to the roof of my mouth, before I sign that." I doubt if there is one here who would sign it. Will you, then, pay no attention to God's invitation? I beg of you, do not make light of it. It is a loving God inviting you to a feast, and God is not to be mocked. Go play with the forked lightning, go trifle with pestilence and disease, but trifle not with God.
> Just let me write out another answer. *"To the King of Heaven: While sitting in Convention Hall, Kansas City, Mo., November 16, 1899, I received a pressing invitation from one of your mes-*

sengers to be present at the marriage supper of
your only begotten Son. I hasten to reply. BY THE
GRACE OF GOD I WILL BE PRESENT."

Who will sign that? Is there one here who will
put his name to it? Is there no one who will say,
"By the grace of God I will accept the invitation
now"? May God bring you to a decision now.
If you would ever see the kingdom of God, you
must decide this question one way or the other.
What will you do with the invitation? I bring it
to you in the name of my Master; will you accept
or reject it? Be wise tonight, and accept the invitation. Make up your mind that you will not
go away till the question of eternity is settled.

Day by day had passed in much the same way
that week. Mr. Moody found it impossible to walk,
although it did not trouble him to stand for an
hour twice daily before those large audiences and
preach. On Thursday he had quite a chill in the
bathroom, and had to summon a doctor on Friday.
Under the doctor's advice he decided to relinquish
all further attempt to proceed with the mission.
With this decision a burden rolled off his mind,
and he began to gain. Steps were taken for his immediate return home.

A beautiful incident occurred on the homeward
journey—illustrative of what used to happen very
frequently of late years, north and south, east and
west, wherever Mr. Moody went on his evangelistic
missions.

When the train pulled into Detroit it was over an
hour late, and unless at least half of this time should
be made up, the eastern connection at Niagara for
the through Boston train could not be made.

While the train was standing in the depot, waiting for the signal to start, someone told the engineer that Mr. Moody was on board.

"Where has he been?" came the question.

"He has been holding meetings in Kansas City, where he was taken ill, and now we are taking him home. We are about an hour late, and if we don't make up the time we won't make the proper connections for Boston."

"Look here," said the engineer, his voice choking as he spoke, "fifteen years ago I was converted by Moody, and I have lived a better and a happier life ever since. I didn't know he was on board tonight, but if you want me to make up the time for you, I'll do it. Just tell him that one of his friends is at the throttle, and then hold your breath."

As soon as the train got clear of the city the engineer pulled open the throttle, and it is said that he make the fastest time ever made over his division. Including stops, he ran one hundred and thirty miles in exactly one hundred and thirty minutes. Connections were made all right, and when the party awakened the next morning they were on the Boston train.

The first intimation of sickness that his family had was a telegram: "Doctor thinks I need rest. Am on my way home." This was followed at short intervals by other telegrams: "Improving rapidly. Have not felt so well for a week"; and "Have had a splendid day; no fever; heart growing better all the time; no pain. Am taking good care of myself, not only for the loved ones, but for the work I think God still has for me to do on earth."

On reaching home, he telegraphed back to Kansas City as follows:

> Have reached home safely. Have traveled backward and forward for forty years, and never stood trip better. Regret exceedingly being forced to leave. Had I been with you tonight, I would have preached on "Thou art not far from the kingdom." My prayer is that many may be led into the kingdom under Mr. Torrey's preaching. I want to thank the good people of Kansas City for their kindness and prayers.

He did not seem to think that he was drawing near his eternal home. He went upstairs that evening to get ready for supper, but the effort expended in climbing the stairs affected his heart so that he was completely exhausted; and he never came downstairs again.

From Sunday, November 19, until Friday, December 22, Mr. Moody was confined to the house. He never complained. Neither he nor his family anticipated the actual outcome. Once he asked if there was plenty of wood and coal in the cellar to carry the household through the winter. Another time he said to his wife that he had never expected a lingering sickness; that he thought his end would come suddenly, owing to heart-failure, while he was in full harness. As time wore slowly away— slowly to a man of such tremendous activity as he— he used to say that every night he longed for the morning. As he grew weaker, he said he now knew what that verse meant, "The grasshopper shall be a burden." But up to 3 A.M. of the day his spirit swept triumphantly within the gates of Heaven, he talked and planned about the future, and never let others know it if he realized what actually did come to pass. His family understood that his heart was weak, but while they knew that the end was possible at any moment, they had no thought that it was probable.

The immediate physical cause of Mr. Moody's breakdown was undoubtedly the fact that he developed fatty degeneration of the heart. During the summer of 1899 circumstances were such that he did not exercise as much as usual, and he increased his weight by thirty pounds. This increase vas fatal to a man of his build, whose heart was so weak. But his enormous vitality, his iron constitution, enabled him to stand a strain under which another would have gone down sooner. Despite the best expert medical assistance, he gradually became weaker and weaker, until the limit of nature was reached, and the Christian world was stunned by the sudden news that he was not, for God had taken him.

Chapter 22

CORONATON DAY

To THE WORLD December 22 was the shortest day of all the year, but for D. L. Moody its dawn ushered in that day that knows no night. For forty-four years he had been a partaker of the divine life, and the transition from the seen to the unseen, from the sphere of the temporal to the eternal, was no interruption in his life. In other realms he continues to serve the same Master whose cause he loved with devotion and served with tireless energy. His one aim in his earthly life had been to do the will of God, and with characteristic readiness he responded to God's last summons.

Until within a few hours of the end, Mr. Moody shared with the family the conviction that he was improving. The day before he had seemed rather more nervous than usual, but spoke cheerfully about himself. In reply to an inquiry if he was comfortable, he said:

"Oh, yes! God is very good to me—and so is my family."

No man loved his family and lifework more devotedly, and frequently he had been heard to say:

"Life is very sweet to me, and there is no position of power or wealth that could tempt me from the throne God has given me."

It was not that he was tired of life and wanted to be done with service that made him so ready to leave, for he knew such joy of Christian service as few have experienced.

The final summons came unexpectedly. During the first half of the night, A. P. Fitt, his son-in-law, had been on duty at his bedside. He slept the greater part of the time. At three in the morning his son, W. R. Moody, took the place as watcher in the sick chamber. For several hours the patient was restless and unable to sleep, but about 6 A.M. he quieted down, and soon fell into a natural sleep.

He awoke in about an hour. His son suddenly heard him speaking in slow and measured words, and he was saying:

"Earth recedes; Heaven opens before me."

His son's first impulse was to try to arouse him from what he thought was a dream.

"No, this is no dream, Will," he said. "It is beautiful! It is like a trance! If this is death, it is sweet! There is no valley here! God is calling me, and I must go!"

Meanwhile the nurse was summoning the family and the physician, who had spent the night in the house. Mr. Moody continued to talk quietly on, and seemed to speak from another world his last messages to the loved ones he was leaving.

"I have always been an ambitious man," he said; "ambitious not to leave wealth or possessions, but to leave lots of work for you to do. You will carry on Mount Hermon; Paul will take up the Seminary, when he is older; Fitt will look after the

Institute; and Ambert [his nephew] will help you all in the business details."

Then it seemed as though he saw beyond the veil, for he exclaimed:

"This is my triumph; this is my coronation day! I have been looking forward to it for years."

Then his face lit up, and he said, in a voice of joyful rapture, "Dwight! Irene! I see the children's faces!" referring to his two little grandchildren, whom God had taken home within the past year.

Then, as he thought he was losing consciousness, he said:

"Give my love to them all."

Turning to his wife, he added:

"Mamma, you have been a good wife to me!"

With this he became unconscious. Up to this time no drugs whatever had been administered.

It seemed to his family that he would never come back again, the sinking was so extreme. In half an hour, however, he revived under the effect of heart stimulants, and as he regained consciousness he feebly uttered these words:

"No pain! No valley!"

Presently, as he rallied further, he added:

"If this is death, it's not bad at all! It's *sweet!*"

A little later, suddenly raising himself on his elbow, he exclaimed:

"What does all this mean? What are you all doing here?"

His wife explained that he had not been as well, and immediately it all seemed to be clear to him, and he said:

"This is a strange thing! I've been beyond the gates of death to the very portals of Heaven, and here I am back again. It is very strange!"

Again he said: "This is my coronation day! It's glorious!" and talked about the work he was leaving behind, assigning to his two sons the Northfield schools, and to his daughter and her husband the Chicago Bible Institute. Asked what his wife's charge would be, he said:

"Oh, Mamma is like Eve, the mother of us all!"

To the urgent plea that he remain longer with his family he said:

"I'm not going to throw my life away. I'll stay as long as God wants me to; but if my time is come, I'm ready."

Something was soon said that showed how clear his mind was. He remarked with deliberation:

"This is the twenty-second of December, isn't it? Five months ago today Irene died . . . and in this room!"

It was actually but four months (since August 22), but anyone might make such a mistake.

Presently a new thought seemed to possess him, as he doubtless felt within him the rallied strength that often just precedes the end, he exclaimed:

"I'm not at all sure but that God may perform a miracle and raise me up. I'm going to get up and sit in the chair. If God wants to heal me by a miracle that way, all right; and if not, I can meet death in my chair as well as here."

Turning to one who was applying warm cloths, he said:

"Here, take those away! If God is going to perform a miracle, we don't want them; and the first thing I suppose we should do will be to discharge you, doctor."

He did not insist on this, however, but could not be dissuaded from getting up. He walked across the room to an easy chair and sat down. A second sinking turn (which lasted only a few moments) left him exhausted, and he was willing to return to bed, where he remained quietly resting and sleeping for over an hour. Another sinking spell of brief duration intervened before the end.

To the very last he was thinking of those about him, and considering them. Turning to his wife, only a little while before he left, he said:

"This is terrible on you, Mamma; it's such a shock. I'm sorry to distress you in this way. Brace yourself. It is hard to be kept in such anxiety."

A few minutes before noon he was evidently sinking once again, and as the doctor approached to administer another hypodermic injection of nitroglycerine, Mr. Moody looked at him in a questioning and undecided way, and said, perfectly naturally:

"Doctor, I don't know about this. Do you think it wise?"

The doctor said he thought it would be all right.

"Well," Mr. Moody said, "it's prolonging the agony for the family!"

The doctor turned away, seeing that the patient's life could not be saved. In a few moments more another sinking turn came on, and from it Mr. Moody awoke in the presence of Him whom he loved and served so long and faithfully. It was not like death, for he fell on sleep quietly and peace-fully, and it was not hard to imagine his reception in that other world among the host of loved ones awaiting his coming. The whole occurrence was such, in the mercy of God, that the substance as well as the sting of death was removed.

A friend wired from a distant city: "Mr. Moody's love for music is at last satisfied this Christmas morning."

Chapter 23

LAID AT REST

D. L. Moody was buried as he died—a victor. There was, indeed, no martial music or stately parade following a plumed hearse. In fact, there was no hearse, no funeral music, no tolling bells, no crepe, no veils to hide faces suffused in tears. Tears were in the eyes of every one of the large congregation that gathered to pay tribute to the dead. But there was no hopeless weeping. Everything was done in as near accord as could be imagined with what Mr. Moody himself would wish.

December 26, 1899, the day of the funeral, was a perfect day—"one of the Lord's own days," a visitor called it. The sun rose clear over the mountain at whose feet Northfield nestles. In the distance, on the foothills of the Green Mountains, patches of snow appeared. The morning was frosty, but in the afternoon, as the friends gathered for the service, the temperature had risen several degrees.

At ten o'clock a brief service was held at the house, conducted by Dr. C. I. Scofield, pastor of the local Congregational church, and R. A. Torrey, pastor of the Chicago Avenue (Moody's) Church, Chicago. Dr. Scofield read the Ninetieth Psalm and the fourth chapter of I Thessalonians, and Mr. Torrey offered prayer.

No signs of mourning appeared about the house; no crepe was seen on the door. The window shutters were all open.

Shortly after eleven o'clock the coffin was carried out of the house. It was a simple cloth-covered coffin, with quiet trimmings and a plate bearing the name and the dates of Mr. Moody's birth and decease:

DWIGHT L. MOODY
1837—1899

The coffin was placed upon a bier and lovingly carried by thirty-two Mount Hermon students to the Congregational church, half a mile away, where the body was laid in state.

Christmas greens festooned the galleries of the church. About the coffin were appropriate floral tributes from friends and from the trustees, faculties, and students of Mr. Moody's several institutions. At the head was a pillow, in which a crown had been worked in white, with a purple ribbon on which the words were seen: "God is calling me." An open Bible, with "Victory. I Corinthians 15: 53-57" on the left side, and "II Timothy 4:7, 8" on the other, rested at the foot. Palms, ferns, laurel, violets, cut-flowers, and callas were placed about the pulpit.

The public service was held at 2:30 P.M. Old associates, neighbors, and relatives had come from far and near. Simple tributes of love and joyous notes of triumphant praise were given by several friends.

In closing, that hymn which Mr. Moody so dearly loved was sung.

After the public service, the coffin was carried by the Mount Hermon students to Round Top, the Olivet of Northfield. A verse of "Jesus, Lover of my soul" was sung, a brief prayer was offered, a last look was taken by his family at the beloved face of husband and father, and the precious form was lowered into the vault, just at the crown of the little hill.

From this place one could see his birthplace, a stone's-throw to the south; his own home for the last twenty-five years, about as far to the west; the Seminary campus, directly north; Camp Northfield, half a mile up the mountain on the east; and the buildings of Mount Hermon School, about four miles distant down the Connecticut Valley.

As Mr. Moody was walking one evening toward the Auditorium with a friend, he sat on the grass of Round Top to rest. Looking out over the beautiful summer landscape spread before them, gilded with the glory of the westering sun, he said:

"I should like to be here when Christ comes back!"

His longing was not gratified during his life, but his earthly tabernacle rests there, awaiting the voice of the archangel and the trump of God.